THE IMPRESSIONISTS

BY

DAVID SPENCE

Studio Manager: Sara Greasley
Editor: Claire Lucas
Production Controller: Ed Green
Production Manager: Suzy Kelly

ISBN-13: 978-1-84898-081-5 pbk
This compilation published in 2009 by *ticktock* Media Ltd

Printed in China
9 8 7 6 5 4 3 2 1

A CIP catalogue record for this book is available from the British Library.

First published in Great Britain as part of the series *Great Artists* in 1998 by *ticktock* Media Ltd,
The Old Sawmill, 103 Goods Station Road, Tunbridge Wells, Kent, TN1 2DP

Picture credits (t=top; b=bottom; c=centre; l=left; r=right; OFC=outside front cover; OBC=outside back cover):

AKG, London: 5bl, 12/13cb, 15tl, 16bl, 16br, 17cb, 17tl, 18br, 18–19ct, 20–21b, 21t, 24tl, 64–65, 66l, 66–67c, 90tl, 90bl, 102r. AKG London/Erich Lessing: 12cl, 13tr, 15br, 20tl, 20bl, 22t, 23t, 28bl, 29bl, 68–69bl, 69br, 72tr. Archive Durand-Ruel: 58–59cb, 90br. Art Institute of Chicago: 33tl, 33br. Art Institute of Chicago/ Bridgeman Art Library, London: 35t. © The Barnes Foundation, Merion, Pennsylvania, USA/ The Bridgeman Art Library: OFCbc. Bibliothèque Nationale of France, Paris: 10tl, 24cb. Bremen/Lauros-Giraudon/Bridgeman Art Library, London: 34tl. Bridgeman Art Library: 7l, 53bl, 54bl, 54tr, 60l, 78br, 94tl, 100–101t, 114t, 114cr, 114bl, 118l, 120tl, 120bl, 120–121t. By permission of The British Library (7857dd,Opp80): 25t.© British Museum: 80tl. Coinman62/Wikimedia Commons: 6lb. Giraudon: 6r, 34–35, 38–39, 40tl, 40bl, 40–41t, 42–43t, 42–43b, 43r, 44cb, 44–45t, 44–45b, 45tr, 46bl, 46–47t, 47cl, 47br, 48bl, 48–49t, 48–49cb, 48tr, 50bl, 50tl, 50–51t, 51cb, 51bl, 51br, 52l, 52–53t, 53br, 54–55c, 55tl, 55r, 56tl, 57bl, 58bl, 58tr, 60–61c, 61tr, 61bl, 61br, 62tl, 62–63cb, 63tr, 66b, 66t, 67r, 68l ,68–69c, 68–69t, 70tl, 70br, 71tl, 71br, 72cl, 772–73b, 73br, 74l, 74br, 74–75ct, 74–75b, 75br, 76tl, 76br, 76bl, 77t, 77tr, 78–79ct, 79br, 80bl, 80–81c, 81br, 81tr, 82tl, 82bl, 82br, 82–83c, 83cb, 83br, 84l, 84ct, 85c, 86bl, 86r, 87tr, 87br, 89t, 91t, 92–93, 94–95c, 96tl, 96–97b, 97t, 97br, 98tl, 98–99b, 98–99t, 100–101b, 102tl, 103r, 104cb, 104–105t, 105bl, 105br, 106bl, 106cl, 106–107t, 107br, 108bl, 108–109b, 109br, 109tr, 110tl, 111, 112tl, 112–113b, 113br, 113t, 115bl, 115c, 115br, 116tl, 116bl, 116–117b, 117t, 117br, 118br, 119bl, 120–121c, 121br, 123b, 125. Peggy Guggenheim Collection, Venice. Photo © AKG London: 122. Holger, Ellgaard/ Wikimedia Commons: 7tc. The J. Paul Getty Museum: 78bl, 89cb. LonganimE/Wikimedia Commons: 6tc. Mary Evans Picture Library: 5tl, 16tl, 22bl, 26tl, 28bl, 32, 33tr. Metropolitan Museum of Art, New York/Bridgeman Art Library, London: 1, 8–9, 11tl, 14tl. Musee du Louvre. Photo © AKG London: 10b. Musee Marmottan, Paris. Photo © AKG London: 4r. Musee Marmottan/Giraudon: 32tl. Musee de l'Orangerie, Paris/Lauros-Giraudon/Bridgeman Art Library, London: 28–29t. Musee d'Orsay, Paris, France/ Giraudon/ The Bridgeman Art Library: OFCl, 23b, 28–29ct. Musee d'Orsay, Paris, France/ The Bridgeman Art Library: OFCbr. Reproduced by courtesy of the Trustees, The National Gallery, London: 26cl. National Gallery, London/Bridgeman Art Library, London: 27t. National Gallery of Scotland, Edinburgh/Bridgeman Art Library, London: 33cl. National Gallery of Washington: 40–41b. Phillips Collection, Washington DC, USA/ The Bridgeman Art Library: OFCtr, 12tr. Photothèque des Musées de la Ville de Paris: 38bl. The Pierpoint Morgan Library/Art Resource, NY (S0109859): 34–35cb. Private Collection/Bridgeman Art Library, London: 14br. Pushkin Museum, Moscow/Bridgeman Art Library, London: 11cr. Rama/ Wikimedia Commons: 4l. Réunion des Musée Nationaux © Photo RMN-Gérard Blot: 56–57cb. Réunion des Musées Nationaux © RMN/R.G.Ojeda: 110cb, 119cr. Réunion des Musées Nationaux © RMN: 85b, 87tl, 88br. Roger-Viollet © Collection Viollet: 99br. Roger Viollet/Frank Spooner Pictures: 11bl. Roger-Viollet © Harlingue-Viollet: 5br. Ann Ronan/Image Select: 78tl, 79cb. Shelburne Museum: 91br. Shutterstock: 6lc, 7cr, 124, 125b, OBC. Tate Gallery (London): 101br, 123tr. Union Centrale des Arts Decortifs: 39r.

Every effort has been made to trace copyright holders, and we apologize in advance for any omissions. We would be pleased to insert the appropriate acknowledgments in any subsequent edition of this publication.

CONTENTS

Introduction
- What is Impressionism? 4
- The Impressionists 5

Timeline 6–7

Monet
- The world of Monet 10–11
- The art of Monet's day 12–13
- Family, friends & others 14–15
- Family fortunes 16–17
- Success 18–19
- What do Monet's paintings say? 20–21
- The cathedral revolution 22–23
- How were the paintings made? 24–25
- Monet's methods 26–27
- Famous images 28–29
- Monet's last obsession 30–31
- The audience for Monet's pictures 32–33
- What the critics say 34–35

Renoir
- The world of Renoir 38–39
- Influences & early works
  - *Romance & Realism* 40–41
  - *Impressionism* 42–43
- Family, friends & others 44–47
- What do Renoir's paintings say?
  - *Paris society* 48–49
- Famous images 50–51
- How were the paintings made?
  - *The dry style* 52–53
- What do Renoir's paintings say?
  - *A new direction* 54–55
- The Bathers 56–57
- How were the paintings made?
  - *The late style* 58–59
- The audience for Renoir's pictures 60–61
- What the critics say 62–63

Degas
- The world of Degas 66–67
- Influences & early works 68–69
- Family, friends & others 70–71
- Distant relations 72–73
- The Flâneur 74–75
- Famous images 76–77
- What do Degas' paintings say? 78–81
- The invisible observer 82–83
- The dancer in focus 84–85
- How were the paintings made? 86–89
- The audience & the critics 90–91

Cézanne
- The world of Cézanne 94–95
- Influences & early works 96–99
- The art of Cézanne's day 100–101
- Family, friends & others
  - *The secret family* 102–103
  - *Friends from Aix* 104–105
- What do Cézanne's paintings say? 106–107
  - *Mont Sainte-Victoire* 108–109
- How were the paintings made?
  - *The structure of things* 110–111
  - *Still life* 112–113
- Famous images 114–115
  - *The Bathers* 116–117
- How were the paintings made?
  - *The Bathers* 118–119
- The audience for the pictures 120–121

Summary
- The influence of the Impressionist movement 122
- Impressionism today 123

Glossary 124–125

Index 126–128

WHAT IS IMPRESSIONISM?

Impressionism was a 19th-century art movement, originating in France. Impressionist paintings are familiar to us today because we are used to seeing them frequently reproduced in books and on posters. It is a style of painting that is still very popular because the viewer can easily understand its content. Impressionist painting is pleasant to look at, with bright summery scenes that are attractive and appealing to the eye. It typically concentrates on the effect of light on a scene or object, using brushstrokes and vibrant colours to reflect the 'impression' of the scene before them.

IMPRESSION, SUNRISE

Claude Monet

MARINONI'S ROTARY PRINTING PRESS

The high speed printing press was fed with continuous paper and sped up the process of reproducing newspapers and journals.

However, to their contemporaries the Impressionist's paintings, with their sketchy unfinished style and modern subject matter, were considered too shocking to be exhibited at the Salon (the official exhibition of the Académie des Beaux-Arts) where the unsuspecting French public might see them. They were not used to seeing such a casual approach to painting. The edge of the canvas cut off the scene at random, as if photographed with a camera, and this new way of painting was challenging to the public not only in the way that it was made but also in what it showed. These paintings included pictures of people living out their daily lives in their own homes, and images of alcoholics and prostitutes – subjects that had previously been considered unfit for the artist to represent.

The technology of the day also had an impact on the development of Impressionism. The growing number of newspapers and journals circulated wider and wider thanks to more efficient and cheaper reproduction methods, and an increasingly literate public were able to read about the latest art, and see reproductions. The movement even owed its name to a journalist – critic Louis Léroy entitled his review 'Exhibition of the Impressionists', after the term used in the title of Monet's painting *Impression, Sunrise* depicting a sunrise over the sea at Le Havre *(above)*.

THE IMPRESSIONISTS

CLAUDE MONET

14 November 1840 –
6 December 1926

Monet's circle of friends included some of the most influential artists of the period. Painting 'en plein air' (outdoors) was at the heart of Impressionism as far as Monet was concerned. He considered it the only way to capture the immediacy of the scene and the changing shades of light and colour.

PIERRE-AUGUSTE RENOIR

25 February 1841 –
3 December 1919

It was while painting with Monet at La Grenouillère in 1869 that Renoir became interested in the effect of light and shadow and the reflections from the water on the surrounding scene. Renoir concentrated on the pleasant side of life, painting scenes from the ordinary everyday world of the Parisian worker at play, and it is this record of real life that makes his painting fascinating.

EDGAR DEGAS

19 July 1834 –
27 September 1917

Degas exhibited paintings with his fellow artists but never considered himself an Impressionist painter. There were considerable differences between his style and that of others, yet he shared their desire to capture movement, and painted exactly what he observed in modern Parisian life. He was a great innovator, experimenting with new techniques to produce the effects on canvas and paper that he was looking for.

PAUL CÉZANNE

19 January 1839 –
22 October 1906

Cézanne was reaching for a way of painting what was beneath the surface, the basic form of his subject expressed and modelled in colour. His fellow Impressionist painters worked very quickly in order to capture the fleeting impression of light on the surface whereas Cézanne worked slowly, laboriously, using colour to build solid shapes.

Camille Pissarro (10 July 1830 – 13 November 1903)
Pissarro is known as the 'Father of Impressionism'. He exhibited at all eight of the Impressionist Exhibitions, and, amongst others mentored Cézanne.

Édouard Manet (23 January 1832 – 30 April 1883)
Manet was considered a key figure in the change from Realist to Impressionist painting styles. He was heavily influenced by the Impressionist painters Claude Monet and Berthe Morisot.

Alfred Sisley (30 October 1839 – 29 January 1899)
Sisley was an Impressionist landscape painter, born in Paris to English parents, he spent most of his time in France, and painted 'en plein air' with Bazille, Monet and Renoir.

Berthe Morisot (14 January 1841 – 2 March 1895)
Morisot had exhibited at the Salon for nearly 10 years before exhibiting with the Impressionists. It was Morisot who convinced Manet to try painting 'en plein air'.

Mary Cassatt (22 May 1844 – 14 June 1926)
Born in America, Cassatt first moved to Paris in 1866. She originally had works exhibited in the Salon, but after an invitation from Degas, exhibited with the Impressionists. Degas had a great influence on Cassatt and introduced her to the art of etching.

TIMELINE

~1830~
- Camille Pissarro – known as the 'Father of the Impressionists' – born 10 July.
- July Revolution leads to crowning of Louis-Philippe *(right)* as 'King of the French'.

~1832~
- Édouard Manet born on 23 January.

~1834~
- Edgar de Gas is born on 19 July.

~1839~
- Paul Cézanne born on 19 January.
- Alfred Sisley born on 30 October.

~1840~
- Inauguration of the Colonne de Juillet (July Column) built in the centre of the Place de Bastille to comemmorate the three days of the July Revolution in 1830 *(right)*.
- Monet born on 14 November.

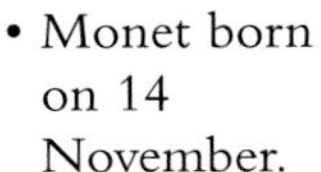

~1841~
- Berthe Morisot born on January 14.
- Renoir born on 25 February.

~1844~
- Mary Cassatt born on 22 May.

~1848~
- French Revolution ends reign of Louis-Philippe – the last king to rule France. Creation of French Second Republic.

~1852~
- Cézanne attends the Collège Bourbon where he meets Émile Zola and Jean Baptiste Baille. The three become best friends.
- Second French Empire established under rule of Emperor Napoleon III.

Coin showing the head of Napoleon III.

~1853~
- Start of Crimean War.

~1854~
- Renoir becomes an apprentice at Levy Brothers, painting plates and vases.

~1856~
- Monet starts drawing lessons.

~1857~
- Cézanne attends the drawing school in Aix.

~1858~
- Renoir made redundant by new technique for printing onto porcelain.

~1859~
- Cézanne attends the University of Aix to study law.
- Monet goes to Paris to study painting, where he meets Camille Pissarro.

~1861~
- Cézanne spends the summer in Paris studying art at the Académie Suisse where he meets Pissarro.
- Cézanne returns to Aix to work in the family bank.

~1862~
- Cézanne gives up work and his legal studies to return to Paris with a modest allowance from his father.
- Renoir studies at Charles Gleyre's studio where he meets Sisley, Monet and Bazille.

~1863~
- Cézanne attends the Académie Suisse once more and meets Impressionist painters Sisley, Monet and Renoir.

~1864~
- Renoir has a painting accepted by the Salon but later destroys it.

~1865~
- Monet shares studio with Bazille where he meets Cézanne and Manet.
- Degas' *The Suffering of the City of New Orleans (below)* is exhibited at the Paris Salon exhibition.

~1866~
- Cézanne submits work to the Paris Salon but is rejected.

~1870~
- Outbreak of Franco-Prussian war.

~1871~
- Monet receives support from dealer Paul Durand-Ruel.
- Establishment of French Third Republic.

~1872~
- Cézanne moves to the village of Auvers-sur-Oise and works with Pissarro.
- Renoir spends the summer painting with Monet. Monet paints *Impression, Sunrise.*

~1874~
- First group exhibition of Impressionist painters. There were 165 works on display at the studio of the photographer Félix Tournachon on the Boulevard des Capucines, from 320 different artists, including Renoir, Monet, Pissarro, Morisot, Degas, Sisley, Boudin and Cézanne.

~1876~

- Second Impressionist Exhibition.
- Renoir paints *Le Moulin de la Galette* which has since become one of the most expensive paintings ever sold.

~1877~

- Third Impressionist Exhibition.

~1878~

- Paris World Fair 'Exposition Universelle' held.

~1879~

- Fourth Impressionist Exhibition.

~1880~

- Fifth Impressionist Exhibition.
- Monet's first one-man exhibition is a success.

~1881~

- Sixth Impressionist Exhibition.
- Degas' sculpture of the *Little Dancer of Fourteen Years* is exhibited.

~1882~

- Seventh Impressionist Exhibition.
- Paul Durand-Ruel exhibits Degas' work in London.

~1883~

- Renoir experiments with new 'Dry Style' of painting.

Renoir's Blonde Bather *was painted in the Dry Style in 1887.*

~1886~

- Eighth Impressionist Exhibition.

~1887~

- Monet's paintings exhibited in New York by Durand-Ruel.
- Eadweard Muybridge publishes his photographic study of movement, *Animal Locomotion.*

~1888~

- The first Kodak camera, developed by inventor George Eastman and pioneering the use of photographic film is made available.

George Eastman, founder of the Eastman Kodak Company.

~1889~

- A record price of 10,000 francs paid for a Monet painting.
- Eiffel Tower built *(right).*

~1891~

- Mrs Potter Palmer pays 5,000 francs for a Degas painting.

~1892~

- Renoir's *Young Girls at the Piano* purchased by the State.

~1893~

- Monet buys land at Giverny to develop water garden.
- Cézanne paints *Rideau, Cruchon et Compotier* which has since become the most expensive Cézanne painting ever to be sold.

~1895~

- Cézanne's first one-man exhibition at the gallery of Ambroise Vollard.
- Lumiere Brothers build a portable movie camera.

~1896~

- Degas buys a Kodak portable camera.

~1899~

- Sisley dies 29 January.

~1900~

- Beginning of Fauvist movement led by Henri Matisse.

~1904~

- Cézanne's works exhibited in Paris and Berlin.
- Signing of Entente Cordiale by Britain and France.

~1905~

- Cézanne exhibits in London.

~1906~

- Cézanne dies on 22 October.

~1907~

- A retrospective exhibition of Cézanne's paintings is held at the Autumn Salon in Paris.
- First Cubist Exhibition held in Paris.

~1911~

- Fogg Art Museum mounts a retrospective of Degas' work.

~1912~

- Louisine Havemeyer pays 478,500 francs for a Degas painting.

~1914~

- It is suggested that Monet paint a large Water Lily Mural for the French State.
- France enters First World War on 3 August.

~1918~

- Armistice declared on 11 November.
- Monet donates eight paintings to the state.

~1917~

- Degas dies on 27 September.

~1919~

- Renoir dies on 3 December.

~1920~

- Monet is offered membership of the 'Institute de France' which is the highest honour the state can bestow on artists – Monet refuses.

~1926~

- Art dealer René Gimpel buys two Monet paintings for 200,000 francs each.
- Monet dies on 6 December.

MONET

THE WORLD OF MONET

THE NOUVELLE-ATHÈNES CAFÉ

Café society was very important to the artist community in Paris. It was in the cafés that they sat and talked, exchanged ideas, and often painted pictures. The Nouvelle Athènes Café became a meeting ground for the Impressionists.

Oscar Claude Monet was born on 14 November 1840 at Rue Lafitte, Paris, the son of a grocer. When he was very young the family moved to Le Havre on the coast in order that Monet's father could join the family wholesale business. Monet's mother died when he was just 17 years old. The only early indication of his artistic leanings were his caricatures which he sold for 10 or 20 francs each. A local artist named Eugène Boudin saw Monet's caricatures displayed in an artist's materials shop and encouraged Monet to paint. Boudin took Monet on painting excursions into the countryside. This *plein air* (open air) method of oil painting was extremely unusual for the time. Monet said *'The fact that I've become a painter I owe to Boudin... I announced to my father that I wanted to become a painter and went off to Paris to study art'.*

THE BEACH AT TROUVILLE *Eugène Boudin*

Boudin was a very influential figure in Monet's life. He met Boudin shortly after the death of his mother, and Boudin taught Monet to paint out of doors directly in front of the subject. Boudin is reported to have told Monet that *'everything that is painted on the spot has a strength, an intensity and a vividness that cannot be recreated in the studio'.*

TERRACE AT SAINTE-ADRESSE, 1867

Monet grew up in and around Le Havre on the Normandy coast. Monet's father joined his brother-in-law's business in Le Havre. The family were prosperous and Monet often visited the family's summer house not far from the seaside town of Sainte-Adresse. Monet painted this picture when he returned there in 1867 and included his father, standing on the terrace, in a scene of such freshness that it is almost possible to feel the breeze which whips the flags.

BOULEVARD DES CAPUCINES, 1873

Monet refused to submit to the formal academic school of training when he went to Paris to study. He could not bring himself to concentrate on the studio drawings from life casts and the official Academy view that reality should be sacrificed to the ideal. Monet quickly began to mix with friends who felt the same as he did about art, such as Auguste Renoir and Alfred Sisley. Monet dressed in style despite being hard up. Renoir stated that *'He was penniless, and he wore shirts with lace cuffs'*. His painting of the *Boulevard des Capucines* was made from the studio of photographer 'Nadar'. It is no coincidence that the picture appears similar to an early photograph with movement captured in the blurred figures that rush by in the street below. Paris must have been an exciting place for the young Monet to live and work, contributing to what art historian E. H. Gombrich has called the 'permanent revolution' in art.

FROZEN IN TIME

The influence of photography was not yet beginning to be felt but the instantaneousness of the photograph, its ability to capture a moment in time, its arbitrary framing of scenes were all qualities that Monet and the other Impressionist painters were seeking in their art.

THE BOATING PARTY LUNCH

Auguste Renoir

Renoir worked with Monet out of doors painting scenes on the river Seine. Monet was to be a strong influence on Renoir, particularly Renoir's use of lighter colours in his paintings. Renoir exhibited at the first three Impressionist exhibitions but eventually his work differed from the Impressionist approach by his use of preparatory drawing and a predetermined colour palette. His efforts to recreate nature using colour resulted in warm and soft pictures, often rose and pink in hue.

ST MARTIN CANAL

Alfred Sisley

Alfred Sisley was of English descent but lived and worked just outside Paris. He devoted himself almost entirely to painting landscapes in the open-air style adopted by the Impressionists. Sisley and Pissarro together with Monet have come to be known as the 'pure' Impressionists, which means that they strived towards naturalism by capturing the fleeting impression of light and its effects, particularly colour and tone, often on the landscape. Sisley went to stay in England during the Franco-Prussian war, painting many scenes from the suburbs surrounding London.

LORDSHIP LANE STATION

Camille Pissarro

Pissarro is the third artist, along with Monet and Sisley, who are considered to be 'pure' Impressionists. Pissarro was born in the West Indies and did not move to Paris until he was 24 years old. He first met Monet in 1859 and his paintings were first exhibited in the Salon des Refusés in 1863 and exhibited with the first Impressionist exhibition in 1874. He painted this picture of Lordship Lane Station in the London suburb of Dulwich in 1871. Pissarro lived in London at the time having escaped from the Franco-Prussian war that was tearing Paris apart. It is said that some 200 paintings left behind in his home in France were used by the invading German soldiers to walk across the muddy garden.

THE ART OF MONET'S DAY

YOUNG WOMAN DRESSED FOR THE BALL

Berthe Morisot

The two best known female Impressionists are Berthe Morisot and Mary Cassatt. Morisot was married to Manet's brother and mixed with the Parisian artist community. She exhibited her paintings at all but one of the Impressionist exhibitions. Women were constrained by social etiquette and it was therefore impossible for them to paint in the open-air manner in the same way as their male counterparts, or deal with the working class subjects covered by the men. Instead what we see in Morisot's work are more domestic interiors and scenes depicting elegant women at leisure.

Monet became good friends with Frédéric Bazille who was studying art in Paris. They shared a studio in the Batignolles quarter of Paris, hence the name given to the Impressionists, the 'Batignolles group'. The aim of all artists, including Monet, was to exhibit work at the Salon. The Salon had existed for over 200 years and was *the* official state gallery, works being selected by the jury of the French Academy of Fine Arts. Its power, however, was fading as the rapidly changing face of art presented new and different works which did not conform to the Academy view. In 1863 the Salon des Refusés exhibited paintings that had been rejected by the jury. This alternative salon was to show more influential paintings than the official Salon but in 1865 Monet had two works accepted by the latter. Édouard Manet came to learn of Monet when the artists' names were confused by the critics. The two artists became friends; they learned from each other, and Monet persuaded Manet to take up open-air painting.

FAMILY, FRIENDS & OTHERS

TERRACE AT SAINTE-ADRESSE

This detail from Monet's painting of 1867 shows Monet's father, Claude Adolphe Monet, standing on the terrace in conversation with a woman holding a yellow parasol, possibly Monet's aunt Madame Lecadre.

The first five years of Monet's life were spent in Paris. His family's move to Le Havre was forced by his father joining brother-in-law Jacques Lecadre's ship chandlery business. Monet's mother died in 1857, when he was 17 years old. Jacques Lecadre died the following year and his childless widow, Monet's aunt, cared for Monet until he left home a year later. Monet moved to Paris in 1859 to study painting. In 1862 he studied under art tutor Charles Gleyre. It was from 1863 onwards that Monet's circle of friends grew to include some of the most influential artists of the period. He lived in the Batignolles quarter and it was in the Café Guerbois in the Rue des Batignolles that he met with fellow artists every Monday night. Monet recollects that '*...Manet invited me to accompany him to a café where he and his friends met and talked every evening after leaving their studios. There I met Fantin-Latour, Cézanne and Degas... the art critic Duranty, Émile Zola... I myself took along Bazille and Renoir. Nothing could have been more stimulating than these debates with the constant clashes of opinions*'.

CAMILLE AND JEAN

Monet's first paintings to include Camille Doncieux were made in 1865 when she was 19 years old. Camille became Monet's mistress and his wife five years later. Their first son, Jean, was born in 1867 and in this double portrait of Camille and Jean, painted in 1873 he would have been about six years old. This picture gave Monet the opportunity to deal with his favourite subject - the effects of light as the sun catches the grass.

STUDIO IN THE BATIGNOLLES QUARTER

Henri Fantin-Latour

Monet first met Bazille at the studio of Charles Gleyre in 1862. Bazille and Monet were to become good friends and in 1865 they shared a studio together at 6 Rue Furstenberg in Paris. Two years later when Monet returned, penniless, to Paris after a stay in Le Havre Bazille again offered a place for Monet to stay. Monet's hopes rested on the exhibition of his large canvas *Women in the Garden* but it was not accepted by the Salon and found no buyers from its place of exhibition in the shop window of the artist's supplier Latouche. Bazille bought the painting from Monet, paying for it in instalments. When the Franco-Prussian war began in 1870 Bazille enlisted in the army and tragically was killed by a Prussian sniper at the age of 29. This group portrait shows Manet (seated) painting Astruc's portrait. Behind them are Zola, Maitre, Bazille, Monet, Renoir and Otto Scholderer.

PORTRAIT OF MADAME GAUDIBERT *(detail)*, 1868

One of Monet's first patrons was the shipowner Gaudibert who was based in Le Havre. Gaudibert supported Monet from as early as 1864, but it was four years later that Monet was commissioned to paint this portrait of Madame Gaudibert.

The Life of Monet

~1840~

Born on 14 November at Rue Lafitte, Paris to Claude Adolphe and Louise Justine Monet.

~1845~

Moves with family to Le Havre.

~1856~

Starts drawing lessons and meets artist Eugène Boudin.

~1857~

Monet's mother dies.

~1859~

Decides to go to Paris to study painting where he meets Camille Pissarro.

~1861~

Called up for military service and sent to Algeria but falls ill and returns to France.

~1865~

Shares studio with Bazille where he meets Cézanne and Manet. Meets Camille Doncieux.

~1867~

Birth of son Jean.

~1870~

Marries Camille. Outbreak of Franco-Prussian war. Monet travels to London.

FAMILY FORTUNES

MONEY FROM SHOPPING

The Hoschedé department-store fortune did not last. Ernest Hoschedé was declared bankrupt in 1877 forcing him to sell his art collection. Ernest died on 18 March 1891 enabling his widow Alice to resolve the ambiguous relationship between the Hoschedé and Monet families. Alice had been Monet's mistress long before they were finally able to be married in 1892. Monet and Alice were together until Alice's death in 1911.

In 1876 after several successful years as an artist, which also included several financial crises, Monet met the department store owner Ernest Hoschedé. Hoschedé was an admirer of Monet and invited him to the Hoschedé estate at the Château de Rottenburg where Monet was given his own studio in the park. Monet was commissioned to produce four decorative paintings for the château. Camille and Jean stayed at home in Argenteuil while Monet was at the château and it may have been during this time, when Monet and Hoschedé's wife Alice spent many an evening together, that they became lovers. Certainly their deep friendship started here. Hoschedé supported many of the Impressionists; when his business ran into trouble in 1878 he was forced to sell all the paintings, causing prices and therefore the market value of their work to fall.

CAMILLE MONET ON HER DEATHBED, 1879

Monet was driven to paint the tragic scene of his wife on her deathbed. He later said *'I caught myself watching her tragic temples, almost mechanically searching for the changing shades which death imposed upon her rigid face. Blue, yellow, grey, whatever… even before the idea had occurred to me to record her beloved features my organism was already reacting to the sensation of colour…'*

PORTRAIT OF GEORGES CLEMENCEAU

(detail), Édouard Manet

The French statesman Georges Clemenceau was a staunch supporter of Monet. Clemenceau ran a magazine entitled *La Justice* which carried many favourable reviews of Monet's paintings and even articles written by Clemenceau himself. He was instrumental in acquiring paintings by Monet for the state, especially after 1907 when he became Prime Minister of France. Clemenceau is perhaps best known for his Treaty of Versailles negotiations after the first world war. This portrait was painted by Monet's friend Édouard Manet in 1880.

JEAN MONET ASLEEP, 1868

When Monet's son, Jean, was 12 years old he inherited six more brothers and sisters. The unhappy financial fortunes of the Hoschedé family meant they were in need of a home. Ernest Hoschedé, his wife Alice and their six children went to live with Claude and Camille Monet, their son Jean and new-born son Michel in a house in the Rue des Mantes in Vétheuil, thirty miles outside Paris. Camille was very ill and it soon became clear she was dying. On 5 September 1879, after a long illness, Camille died. After her death Monet's sons Jean and Michel were brought up by Alice Hoschedé alongside her own children.

OPEN AIR STUDY - WOMAN TURNED TO THE LEFT

The model for this *plein air* study, made in 1886, is thought to be Monet's step-daughter, Suzanne Hoschedé. Suzanne married the American artist Theodore Butler in 1892 but died suddenly in 1899. Monet and Suzanne's mother Alice were deeply affected by her death.

THE LIFE OF MONET

~1871~
Monet's father dies and he travels to Holland. He receives support from dealer Paul Durand-Ruel.

~1874~
First group Impressionist exhibition.

~1876~
Becomes friends with Alice and Ernest Hoschedé. Camille falls ill.

~1878~
Second son Michel is born.

~1879~
Camille dies. Fourth Impressionism exhibition held.

~1880~
Monet's first one-man exhibition is a success.

~1887~
Monet's paintings exhibited in New York by Durand-Ruel.

~1889~
A record price of 10,000 francs paid for a Monet painting.

~1892~
Marries Alice Hoschedé.

~1893~
Buys land at Giverny to develop water garden.

~1911~
Alice Hoschedé dies.

~1912~
Doctors diagnose cataracts in both of Monet's eyes.

SUCCESS

Monet became famous in his own lifetime. The early years were a struggle with money in short supply but eventually he found patrons willing to support him. It is true to say that life was never as hard for Monet as it was for some artists, Vincent van Gogh for example, but his commitment to his art was absolute. Monet was enjoying a degree of success while in his forties and by the time he was in his fifties his recognition was such that American artists went to Giverny to be near him, resulting in one, Theodore Butler, actually marrying into the Monet family. As a result of this widespread recognition there exist today many records of interviews with Monet as well as articles, reviews and family memoirs.

MADAME CLAUDE MONET WITH HER SON JEAN IN THE GARDEN AT ARGENTEUIL

Auguste Renoir

One of Monet's recollections described a visit by Manet in 1874 when Auguste Renoir was staying with Monet at Argenteuil. Monet's wife Camille and son Jean were sitting in the garden. All three artists set up their easels to paint the scene. *'One day, excited by the colours and light, Manet started an open air study of figures under trees. While he was working, Renoir came along. He too was captured by the mood of the moment. He asked me for palette, brush and canvas, sat down next to Manet and started painting. Manet watched him out of the corner of his eye and now and again went over to look at his canvas… he tiptoed over to me and whispered "The lad has no talent. Since you are his friend tell him he might as well give up."'*

THE GARE SAINT-LAZARE

Monet knew the Gare Saint-Lazare well as it was from here that he took the train to both Argenteuil and Le Havre. In 1877 Monet exhibited seven views of the station along with other works in a show of group Impressionist works. The story of how Monet came to paint these pictures is recounted by Jean Renoir:

'One day he said "I've got it! The Gare Saint-Lazare! I'll show it just as the trains are starting, with smoke from the engines so thick you can hardly see a thing. It's a fascinating sight, a dream world." He did not of course intend to paint it from memory. He would paint it in situ *so as to capture the play of sunlight on the steam rising from the locomotives.*

'I'll get them to delay the train for Rouen half an hour. The light will be better then.'

Renoir told him he was mad. Monet went to see the director of the Western Railway and explained that he wanted to paint either the Gare du Nord or Gare Saint-Lazare but *'...yours had more character.'* The overawed director consented, instructing the engine driver to make steam while Monet sat and painted. Renoir finished the story by saying, *'I wouldn't have dared to paint even in front of the corner grocer!'*

The Life of Monet

~1914~

Eldest son Jean dies. It is suggested that Monet paint a large Water Lily Mural for the French State. France enters First World War on 3 August.

~1915~

Monet builds a new studio over 23 metres long to paint *Water Lily* mural.

~1918~

Armistice declared on 11 November. Monet donates eight paintings to the state, chosen by Prime Minister Clemenceau.

~1920~

Monet is offered membership of the 'Institute de France' which is the highest honour the state can bestow on artists. Monet refuses.

~1923~

Regains his eyesight after an operation on cataracts.

~1925~

Burns some of his paintings as they do not meet his own high expectations.

~1926~

Art dealer René Gimpel buys two paintings for 200,000 francs each. Monet dies on 6 December.

WHAT DO MONET'S PAINTINGS SAY?

THE BASIN AT ARGENTEUIL, 1872

Monet chose Argenteuil as his new home, moving to a rented house with his young family. Argenteuil was a small town which lay on the right bank of the Seine just six miles from the main Saint-Lazare railway station in Paris. From the 1850s the impact of the railway line was changing the provincial towns surrounding Paris. It enabled Parisians to make day trips to the rural areas, as well as enabling those living in the towns to commute to Paris. The railway also had the effect of stimulating industrial growth away from Paris and factories were beginning to be built in the first stages of urban and suburban sprawl. Monet painted many views of the Seine and countryside surrounding his new home.

This view shows families strolling along the river bank. The broken sunlight falls through the trees creating an ideal subject for Monet's brush – the perfect rural idyll. Monet would spend a very productive and happy six years at his home in Argenteuil.

In 1866 Monet painted a picture of the 19-year-old Camille Doncieux. Camille became Monet's favourite model and also his mistress. Monet's father disapproved and cut off his son's allowance. At the same time Monet suffered the blow of rejection of his big painting *Women in the Garden* by the Salon jury. In addition Camille was pregnant and their son, Jean, was born on 8 August 1867. Fearful of the impending war with Prussia they moved to Trouville on the Normandy coast, and subsequently to London and Holland. During this period Monet's struggle to make pictures which would be accepted by the Salon and to establish his career underwent a change. When Monet returned to Paris after the war his commitment to *en plein air* painting was greater than ever. When Boudin saw the paintings Monet brought back from his travels he commented *'I think he's got all the makings and is going to be the leader of our movement'.*

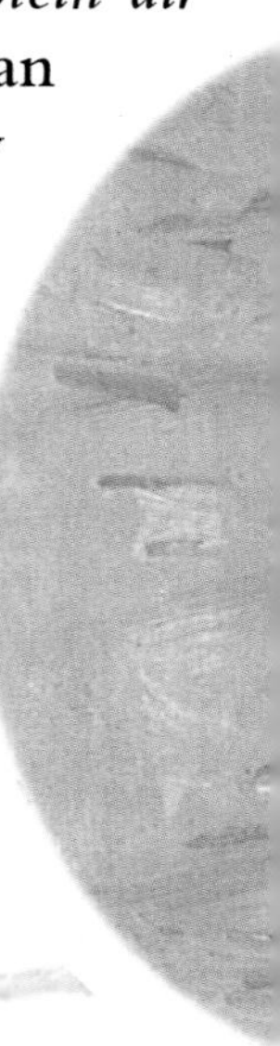

IMPRESSION, SUNRISE, 1872

By 1872 Monet had become disenchanted with the Salon exhibition and had not entered any paintings for consideration. A group of independent painters including Monet, Renoir, Sisley, Degas, Cézanne, Pissarro and Morisot decided to organize their own exhibiting society. On 23 December 1873 the 'Société Anonyme Coopérative d'Artistes Peintres, Sculpteurs, Graveurs' was founded. An exhibition was planned for April 1874 to be held in the studios of the photographer Félix Tournachon (known as Nadar) on the Boulevard des Capucines. Monet showed nine pictures, including *Impression, Sunrise.*

THE IMPRESSIONISTS

A review of the exhibition by Louis Leroy in the satirical magazine *Le Charivari* has become famous. He entitled the review 'Exhibition of the Impressionists' and so claimed responsibility for naming the movement *Impressionism*. Leroy wrote the review in the manner of two visitors discussing the exhibition:

'What is this a painting of? Look in the catalogue.'
'Impression, Sunrise.'
'Impression - I knew it. I was just saying to myself, if I'm impressed, there must be an impression in there… and what freedom, what ease in the brushwork! Wallpaper in its embryonic state is more finished than this seascape!'

The painting which caused the sensation was of a sunrise over the sea at Le Havre. It was nothing new for Monet. In this picture as in others he strived to create an impression of a rapidly changing scene as the orange sunlight reflected on the shimmering water.

Rouen Cathedral

THE CATHEDRAL REVOLUTION

'Professionals will please excuse me, but I cannot resist the desire to establish myself as an art critic for a day. It's Claude Monet's fault. I entered Durand-Ruel's gallery to take a leisurely look again at the studies of the cathedrals of Rouen, which I had enjoyed seeing at the Giverny studio. And that's how I ended up taking that cathedral with its manifold aspects away with me, without knowing how. I can't get it out of my mind. I'm obsessed with it. I've got to talk about it. And for better or worse, I will talk.' **Georges Clemenceau wrote these words in 1895, eleven years before he was elected Prime Minister of France. Clemenceau's great support for Monet helped consolidate the artist's reputation. In 1907, the year after Clemenceau was elected, the state bought one of the Rouen Cathedral paintings for the home of government in Paris, the Palais de Luxembourg.**

ROUEN CATHEDRAL, PORTAL, MORNING SUN, HARMONY IN BLUE

In February 1892 Monet rented a room opposite Rouen cathedral. After painting the view of the cathedral several times he changed rooms so as to shift his angle of view slightly. After painting this new view he moved again, and again after more pictures. In all he appears to have changed his viewing angle five times, searching for new highlights and shadows as the sunlight fell across the front of the building. In the three paintings illustrated here Monet explores the effect of light at different times of day and in different weather conditions.

ROUEN CATHEDRAL, PORTAL, FULL SUNLIGHT, HARMONY IN BLUE AND GOLD

The early morning cool blues observed in the first painting, *Morning Sun, Harmony in Blue* give way in this painting to the warm golds of the full mid-day sun. The early morning mist has cleared to reveal the front of the cathedral. The deep shadows throw the building into sharp relief. Monet painted 31 pictures of the facade of Rouen cathedral. When he exhibited them at Durand-Ruel's gallery in 1895, priced at 12,000 francs, they were a great success.

ROUEN CATHEDRAL, PORTAL, GREY WEATHER, HARMONY IN GREY

In this third picture Monet explores the same subject in overcast weather. There is no direct sunlight and therefore no deep shadow, instead the cathedral stone is much flatter and more evenly coloured. The aims Monet had for his earlier series of paintings on grain stacks are the same as the aims for the cathedral series: *'I'm plugging away at a series of different effects but the sun goes down so quickly at this time of year that I can't keep up with it… the more I do, the more I see what a lot of work it takes to render what I am looking for, instantaneity, above all the* enveloppe, *the same light diffused everywhere'.*

HOW WERE THE PAINTINGS MADE?

The range of colours employed by artists today has hardly changed from those being used in the 1870s. The development of new colour pigments and stable chemical compounds was the result of new developments in the expanding industries of France and Germany. The new colours were chiefly developed for the painting, decorating and coach-building trades, but the artist's merchants benefited from the same discoveries. Impressionists such as Monet made full use of these colours. The invention of the collapsible tin paint tube in 1841 by the American painter John Rand had expanded the market for pre-ground colours available over the counter. By the 1870s it was commonplace for artists to get their paints in tin tubes from a widening selection of colour pigments. Some artists still preferred to grind the pigment themselves, mixing the powders into paste with the addition of poppy oils, but most were content to do away with this chore.

CHEVREUL'S COLOUR CIRCLE

In 1839 Michel Chevreul, a Director of Dyeing at the Gobelins tapestry workshop, formulated his law of simultaneous contrast of colours. This stated something that artists had known for centuries but had never been scientifically expressed: colours placed next to each other had an effect on how each was perceived. When complementary colours are contrasted the effect is most intense. For example, a red next to its complementary colour, green, makes the red appear redder; similarly the green will appear greener.

The other fundamental complementary colours are orange and blue, and violet and yellow. Monet used this effect to its full in his painting. He said *'...colour owes its brightness to force of contrast... primary colours look brightest when they are brought into contrast with their complementaries'.* Nowhere is this demonstrated better than in Monet's famous painting *Impression, Sunrise (detail above).*

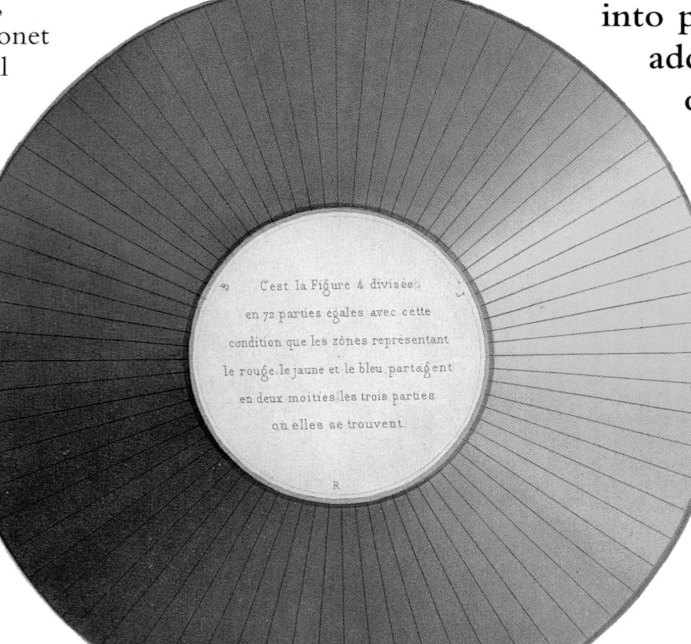

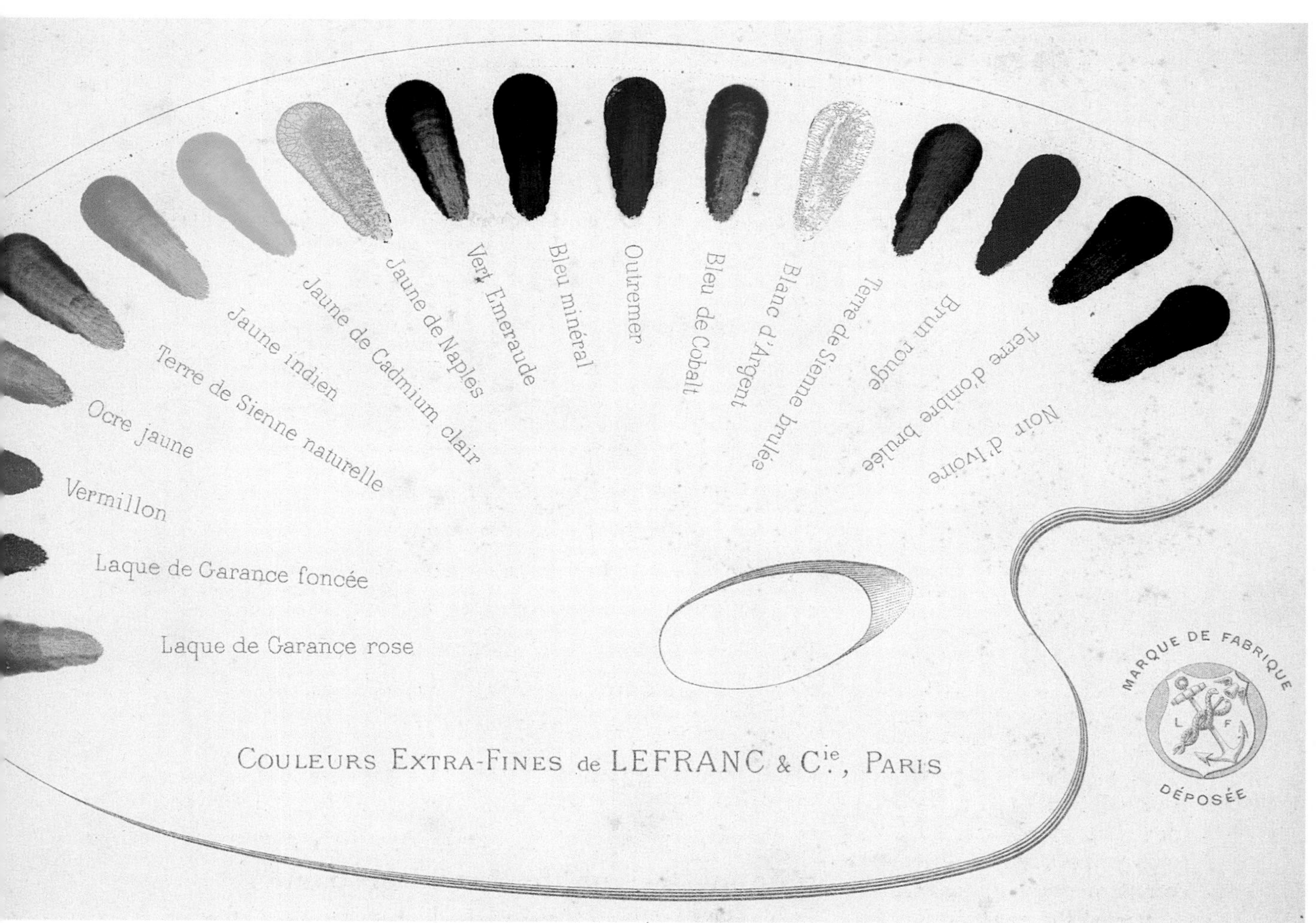

SAMPLE OF LEFRANC & COMPANY'S OIL PAINTS

The Impressionists embraced the new colours that were becoming available. Their obsession with capturing the changing effects of light upon their *motif* meant that they welcomed any scientific advances that could help them in their work. Lefranc sold paint to both the retail and wholesale trades, offering colours ground and unground, mixed with oils for artists. Lefranc even sold empty tin tubes, and pliers to close the tubes. Monet is known to have had colours specially hand ground for him by the colour merchant Mulard in the rue Pigalle.

PORTABLE OIL PAINTS

The collapsible tube was made initially from lead or tin but it was found that lead reacted with chemicals in some paints, so tin became the preferred material. The invention of the tube freed the artist from the studio as never before; when paints suddenly became easily transportable, artists were able to work out of doors. Another benefit was that the life of the paint was extended. The previous method of storing paint was to keep it in a small sack (made from pig's bladder) which the artist would puncture with a tack, squeezing out the paint when required; but the paint would harden quickly.

ILLUSTRATED

Paris Fashions

— The Very Latest —

FRESH AIR IS FASHIONABLE

MONET'S METHODS

The Impressionists made *plein air* or open-air painting famous but there was a tradition of painting out of doors in the 19th century. Monet's commitment to it was such that he even dug a trench into which a large canvas could be lowered in order to work on the top portion of the picture without having to change his viewpoint. He worked directly on the canvas, without the normal preparatory drawings, and would be careful to wear dark clothing in order not to reflect light onto the canvas. The sunshade was essential. Without shade the artist would not be able to get the right colours or tones in the glare of the sun. There were other problems. Berthe Morisot complained that *'...the moment I set up my easel more than fifty boys and girls were swarming about me... this ended in a pitched battle...'*

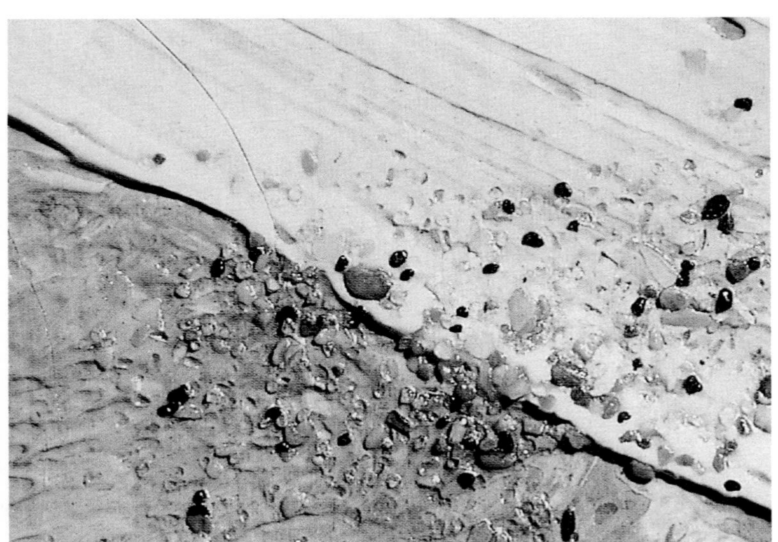

THE EVIDENCE

A magnified view of the painting, revealing sand stuck to the surface, is testimony to the *plein air* nature of its execution.

DETAIL OF WHITE DRESS

Impressionism is well known for an effect known as the *tache,* which is a coloured stroke or 'patch'. This was an artistic development thought to have been made more widespread in the 19th century by the introduction of the flat, square brush as opposed to the round brush. It can be seen quite clearly here in this detail.

Flat ferrule brush

THE BEACH AT TROUVILLE, 1870

The scene Monet depicts probably shows Camille, seated on the left wearing a flowered hat, with Madame Boudin in the dark dress. This was painted shortly after Monet and Camille's marriage on 28 June 1870, as it is known that they stayed at Trouville during the summer. Their son, Jean, was three years old at the time and it could be his shoe that Monet shows casually hanging on the back of the chair. When Monet painted *The Beach at Trouville* he was preoccupied with the effects of changing light. The problems this presented could not have been greater than on the coast with sand reflecting the glare of the sun and very little in the way of shade. It was painted on the beach, and would have taken less than half an hour if we are to believe his statement that '*...no painter could paint more than one half hour on any outdoor effect and keep the picture true to nature...*' although it is possible he returned to the same canvas later.

He had a grooved box built to take wet canvases so he could put one away and take out another, working on several at a time. In order to capture the fleeting effect of the light Monet had to work fast. *'The first painting should cover as much of the canvas as possible, no matter how roughly, so as to determine at the outset the tonality of the whole.'*

FAMOUS IMAGES

Many of Monet's paintings are familiar to us today because we are used to seeing them reproduced so many times in books and for other purposes. Impressionist paintings are probably the most popular of all; it is an easily understood art which does not ask the viewer to work hard to understand the imagery. Impressionist painting is 'comfortable' to look at, its summer scenes and bright colours are appealing to the eye. It is important to remember, however, that this new way of painting was challenging to its public not only in the way that it was made but also in what it showed. They had never seen such 'informal' paintings before. The edge of the canvas cut off the scene in an arbitrary way, as if snapped with a camera.

The subject matter included intimate domestic scenes; pictures of alcoholics; pictures of prostitutes. Never before had these subjects been considered fit for artists. When Monet set about making his paintings he was venturing into unknown territory.

LA RUE MONTORGEUIL
ON 30 JUNE 1878

In 1877 Monet had moved back to Paris, staying at an apartment on the rue d'Edimbourg. It was here that Michel, Monet's second son, was born on 17 March 1878. On 30 June 1878 a public holiday was declared for the World's Fair. The festival was a big occasion with Parisian streets decorated with flags. Monet made two street paintings. He later said *'On 30 June, the first national holiday, I went out with my painting equipment to Rue Montorgeuil; the street was decked out with flags and the crowd was going wild. I noticed a balcony and I went up and asked permission to paint, which was granted. I came down again incognito'.*

THE POPPY FIELD AT ARGENTEUIL, 1873

Painted in 1873 when he was living in Argenteuil with Camille and their son Jean, this picture represents one of the happiest periods in Monet's life. The picture shows two pairs of figures, both comprising a woman and child. It is likely that one couple is Camille and Jean, who would have been five years old when the picture was made. Monet was relatively secure financially although not well off. The previous year had been a success with the Parisian art dealer Paul Durand-Ruel purchasing many paintings. This, in addition to his father's inheritance, made it possible for them to rent in this rural suburb of Paris. The idyllic scene is at the heart of the appeal of Impressionist painting; a warm sunlit summer's day in a field populated with brilliant red poppies. Monet demonstrates awareness of the contrast of colours effect, placing the dabs of red in a ground of green.

WOMEN IN THE GARDEN, 1866

Édouard Manet's painting *Déjeuner sur l'Herbe* when first exhibited to the public in 1863 caused a scandal. Monet was inspired by this work and in 1865 planned a painting on the same subject but this time to be a truthful depiction of modern life, rejecting references to art history (Manet's painting was full of art historical references) and painted with natural light *en plein air.* The picture would be huge, including twelve life-size figures, and would take the 1866 Salon by storm. The picture was never finished, was partially destroyed and cut up into sections which were displayed as paintings in their own right. In 1866 Monet embarked upon an even more daring painting - *Women in the Garden.* For this picture he made no preparatory sketches. Monet worked directly on a canvas two and a half by over two metres in size, working out of doors. It was for this picture that Monet dug a trench, lowering the painting rather than changing his own viewpoint on the subject, so concerned was he to recreate exactly what he saw. Eventually Monet conceded defeat and finished the canvas in his studio.

MONET'S LAST OBSESSION

The water lily paintings are often considered by art historians to be the greatest paintings of Monet's career. In 1883 he rented a house at Giverny, 50 miles from Paris. Seven years later he purchased the house and shortly afterwards, in 1893, purchased a meadow near the property which contained a pond fed by the Ru River, a tributary of the Seine. He employed at least six gardeners who gradually shaped the meadow into a garden of willows, irises and water lilies specially imported from Japan. Monet painted the gardens around the house and then concentrated on the water gardens, painting them repeatedly between 1897 and his death in 1926.

MONET PAINTING WATER LILIES

This photograph shows Monet in his studio. He is holding a palette and is standing in front of one of his vast water lily canvases. In later years Monet depended more and more on his daughter-in-law Blanche who became his continual companion. Her support was important during this time when he was diagnosed as having cataracts and was frightened of going blind. Monet finally had an operation in 1923 after losing all sight in his right eye. Monet had a large studio built in his garden, measuring 12 by 24 metres, enabling him to paint his huge water lily canvases.

MORNING WITH WEEPING WILLOWS, 1916-26

The vast canvases that Monet painted towards the end of his life are considered today to be important works in the development of modern art. *Morning with Weeping Willows* is made up of three sections (the complete middle section and part of each end panel are shown here, each measuring approximately 2 by 4 metres. The paintings represent not just what was in front of Monet's eyes but equally a summary of his sensations. Monet was releasing himself from the representation of a scene in order to synthesize the recollections, impressions and sensations that it generated. The 'abstract' qualities of colour and shape were the dominant consideration. Monet emphasized this by combining into a single painting panels of different views that had been painted at different times in different conditions of light. Monet said of these pictures *'I waited for the idea to take shape, for the groupings and composition of themes to slowly sort themselves out in my brain'*. *Morning with Weeping Willows*, part of a donation to the French state at the end of the First World War, was finally unveiled at the Orangerie in Paris in May 1927, five months after Monet's death.

THE WATER LILY POND, HARMONY IN GREEN, 1899

Monet had an arched wooden bridge built across the narrowest part of the pond. He also had to control the flow of the Ru River to raise the temperature of the water in order that the imported water lilies might thrive. This caused the locals of Giverny to protest. The River Ru was used by the local population for their washing and they thought that Monet's 'Japanese Garden' would pollute their water. In 1901 Monet admitted *'These landscapes of water and reflections have become an obsession'*. A gardener was employed to maintain the water lilies in such a way as to suit Monet's paintings.

THE AUDIENCE FOR MONET'S PICTURES

THE DRAMATIST LOUIS FRANÇOIS NICOLAIE

This caricature was drawn by the Monet at the age of 18.

Monet's first sales were of his caricatures. His talent for caricaturing those around him started at school with sketches of his teachers. Monet said of caricature '*...I quickly developed a skill for it. At the age of 15, I was known all over Le Havre as a caricaturist... I charged for my portraits at 10 or 20 francs per head... had I carried on I would have been a millionaire by now*'. His earliest serious patron was shipowner Gaudibert when Monet was in his early twenties. Some patrons, such as the department store owner Ernest Hoschedé, gave invaluable financial support but the most important figure to support Monet and the Impressionist painters was art dealer Paul Durand-Ruel. Durand-Ruel bought their paintings from the early 1870s and was responsible for showing Impressionism to an international audience in galleries in London and New York. The American patrons became very important to the commercial success of Impressionism. As the paintings became known, American critics and artists followed the fortunes of artists working in France such as Monet.

IMPRESSING AMERICA

In 1870 Monet was staying in London. It was here that he was introduced to Paul Durand-Ruel who had moved his gallery temporarily to London because of the Franco-Prussian war. Monet recalled that '*...without Durand we would have starved like all Impressionists. We owe him everything... he risked everything more than once to support us*'. In 1886 Durand-Ruel organized an exhibition of Impressionist art at the American Art Association in New York. This included 49 works by Monet and was a great success. The following year more Monet paintings were exhibited at the National Academy of Design in New York and the Royal Society of British Artists in London.

NEW YORK OFFICE,
315 FIFTH AVENUE (COR. 32D STREET).

April 12th, 1893.

M. A. Ryerson Esq.,
to
Messrs. Durand-Ruel.

341 - "L'Ile de la Grande Jatte" - $300.
441 - "Place de la Concorde" - 300.
339 - "Le Pont d'Austerlitz" - 350.
440 - "Pont de Notre Dame" - 300.
434 - "La Seine à St. Mammes" - 350.
917 - "Aprèsmidi de Septembre" - 450.
976 - "Meule, effet de neige" - 1,500. $3,550.

Messrs. Durand-Ruel
to
M. A. Ryerson Esq.

- $ 450.

No.2366

Balance in favor of Messrs. Durand-Ruel = $3,100.

ans Shipped besides.

SALES RECEIPT FOR IMPRESSIONIST PAINTINGS

This receipt dated 12 April 1893 itemizes paintings purchased by the wealthy American collector Martin Ryerson from Paul Durand-Ruel's New York office. It includes the picture *Meule, Effet de Neige* by Monet as well as works by Lepine and Sisley. The success of Impressionism in America helped Durand-Ruel establish his New York office on prestigious 5th Avenue.

A PHOTOGRAPH OF CLAUDE MONET, TAKEN AROUND 1904

GRAIN STACK, SNOW EFFECT, OVERCAST WEATHER

This painting is from the series of 15 paintings produced by Monet in 1890 and 1891 which explored the same subject time and again in different light conditions. The French title, *Meule, Effet de Neige, Temps Couvert* can be seen on the Durand-Ruel receipt with some variation.

MARTIN RYERSON WITH CLAUDE MONET

This photograph shows Ryerson with Monet in the garden at Giverny. Ryerson was an important collector of art who later became a founding trustee of the Art Institute of Chicago. Partly because of Ryerson's interest the Art Institute of Chicago now holds one of the most important collections of Impressionist paintings in the world.

CAMILLE, OR THE WOMAN IN THE GREEN DRESS, 1866

In 1865 Monet painted several pictures featuring the young model Camille Doncieux. One picture, called *Camille*, or *The Woman in the Green Dress*, attracted a great deal of attention at the Salon where it was hung. Émile Zola published an article in the daily newspaper *L'Événement* entitled 'The Realists at the Salon'. It read *'I confess the painting that held my attention the longest is* Camille *by M. Monet. Here was a lively energetic canvas. I had just finished wandering through those cold and empty rooms, sick and tired of not finding any new talent, when I spotted this young woman, her long dress trailing behind, plunging into a wall as if there were a hole there. You cannot imagine what a relief it is to admire a little, when you're sick of splitting your sides with laughter and shrugging your shoulders'.*

WHAT THE CRITICS SAY

The eighth and last Impressionist exhibition took place in 1886. Monet could not be persuaded to take part in this show because of the differences that had grown between him and some of his fellow artists. Degas, always quick to argue, criticized Monet's work as superficially decorative. Degas exhibited 15 pastel pictures of women bathing at the final Impressionist exhibition which was dominated stylistically by Pointillist works such as those of Seurat and Signac. These 'neo-impressionistic' paintings based on scientific colour principles found no sympathy with Monet who turned his back on the new developments to concentrate on his own individual style. In the early days of Impressionism it was the establishment in the form of the official Salon and public opinion which had criticized Monet's work. By 1886 his painting was becoming a critical and commercial success and Monet found that the new 'establishment' of the Impressionist exhibitions were being challenged by the scientific objectivity of the Pointillists and the aim of Cézanne *'...to make something solid of Impressionism'.* Art historians have over the course of the last 100 years weighed the relative merits of the Impressionists, neo-Impressionists and those that followed such as Cézanne. As critical fashions change so Monet's work becomes sometimes more, sometimes less, important and influential than those around him.

THE MASTERPIECE

The writer Émile Zola had been very supportive of the new art of Impressionism. In 1886 however he published a book entitled *L'Oeuvre* (The Masterpiece) which casts its leading character, artist Claude Lantier, as a failed dreamer. Several of Zola's friends thought the fictional Lantier was based upon themselves, particularly Cézanne who had until that point been a good friend of Zola. Monet wrote to fellow artist Pissarro *'Have you read Zola's book? I am afraid it will do us a lot of harm'.*

SUNDAY AFTERNOON ON THE ISLAND OF LA GRANDE JATTE

Georges Seurat

This Seurat painting, exhibited at the final Impressionist show of 1886, is typical of the Pointillist style that challenged Monet's Impressionism. Under the influence of colour theorists such as Chevreul the Pointillists applied dots of colour scientifically in order that colours are mixed in the viewer's eye rather than actually on the canvas.

CAMILLE, OR THE CAVERN

caricaturist Bertall

This caricature was drawn by Charles d'Arnoux who published under the pseudonym Bertall. It was published in the weekly satirical magazine *Le Journal Amusant*. Paintings hanging in the Salon exhibition were ruthlessly caricatured for the amusement of the French public regardless of the fame of the artist. The title for this caricature refers to the dark background against which the figure of Camille is depicted.

RENOIR

THE WORLD OF RENOIR

Detail showing Renoir's portrait.

Pierre Auguste Renoir was born in Limoges, France, on 25 February 1841. His father, Leonard Renoir, was a tailor; his mother, Marguerite Merlet, a dressmaker. The family moved to the Louvre area of Paris when Pierre was just four years old, making a home at 23 rue d'Argenteuil. Leonard, Marguerite and their five children shared the Paris apartment which Renoir later recalled as the size of a 'pocket handkerchief'. Leonard continued his business as a tailor from the Rue d'Argenteuil apartment, his tailor's bench being transformed into his own bed at night. Renoir was the second youngest so gradually, as his elder brothers Henri and Victor found jobs and moved out of the family home, the pressure on space eased. The family lived in the very centre of Paris and could observe from their windows the riots of 1848 which led to the Revolution, which in turn installed Louis Napoleon Bonaparte as President of the Republic of France and then Emperor. Renoir grew up in a city being transformed by revolutions of state, industry and, most importantly of all, culture.

PORTRAIT OF 43 PAINTERS IN THE STUDIO OF GLEYRE, *c.*1862

In 1862, at the age of 21, Renoir was accepted at the École des Beaux-Arts to study art. He was an average pupil, frustrated, as many of the students were, by the unadventurous traditional teaching methods with their dependence on studies from models of antiquity. From 1861 Renoir had attended classes in the private studio of the Swiss painter, Charles Gleyre. Many young hopefuls were attracted to Gleyre's style of teaching which was far more liberal than the established schools despite the fact that Gleyre's own painting did not manage to raise itself above the average. Renoir's fellow pupils included Claude Monet, Alfred Sisley and the talented Frédéric Bazille who was tragically to die in the Franco-Prussian war. This group portrait picture of 43 painters in Gleyre's studio includes a portrait of Renoir, painted by his friend Emile-Henri Laporte.

BATHERS IN THE SEINE (LA GRENOUILLÈRE), 1869

This painting by Renoir is one of four he made of the subject. He painted the scene *en plein-air* (outdoors) on site. Claude Monet was another painter of the time who went to La Grenouillère to paint. Monet described his plans in a letter to Bazille; *'I have a dream, a picture, the bathers at La Grenouillère. I have done some poor sketches for it, but it is only a dream. Renoir, who has just spent two months here, also wants to paint this motif.'*

THE ISLAND BAL DE LA GRENOUILLÈRE

The bathing pools at La Grenouillère, just 20 minutes by train from the central Paris station of Saint-Lazare, were a popular day trip destination for Parisians relaxing on weekends or holidays. Although La Grenouillère translates as 'frog-pond' the name had nothing to do with amphibians. 'Frogs' was the name given by men to the girls who spent the summers at the pools and who had a reputation for being flirtatious. Renoir described the 'frogs' as being *'very good sorts'* and found several models who would pose for him among the bathers at La Grenouillère.

THE PORCELAIN PAINTER

At the age of 13 Renoir was apprenticed to a porcelain painter who decorated vases and plates. His brother, Henri, was already established as an engraver and Renoir's family encouraged their children in their artistic trades, eager no doubt to see some money coming in to the family home. Renoir experimented with decorative painting on fans and furniture as well as porcelain. This vase, painted by Renoir when he was an apprentice, is decorated with figures based on Jean Goujon's *Nymphs.*

INFLUENCES & EARLY WORKS:

ROMANCE & REALISM

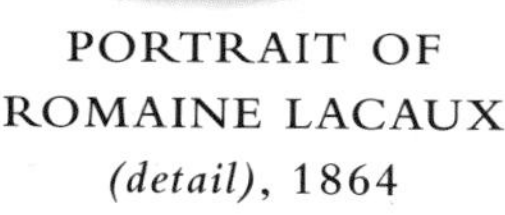

PORTRAIT OF ROMAINE LACAUX *(detail)*, 1864

This portrait of the daughter of a porcelain manufacturer is one of Renoir's earliest commissioned paintings, as well as one of his most accomplished. Painted when he was only 24 years old, Renoir has managed to capture the freshness of youth and clear-eyed innocence of the young Romaine.

Renoir's grounding in painting began as a commercial artist painting figures and scenes on porcelain until this craft was made redundant by the introduction of machine printing. This early experience of copying classical figures and rococo scenes helped Renoir acquire skills which he retained all his working life, as well as developing a lasting interest in the work of the classical masters. His early career as a painter, however, began with his studentship under Charles Gleyre, and continued with his admiration of the works of 19th-century French artists Eugène Delacroix and Gustave Courbet. In 1848 Courbet had caused a stir in the art world with his realistic paintings depicting simple everyday scenes, such as peasants breaking stones for road mending. This realism reflected Courbet's view of the world and art's place within it, and was a break from the traditional subjects thought suitable for art, such as scenes from antiquity painted in a formal classical style. Courbet's break with convention made it possible for artists such as Édouard Manet to concentrate on realistic scenes, and began to free artists from the tyranny of tradition.

WOMEN OF ALGIERS

Eugène Delacroix

Delacroix was considered a great artist even in his own time. His painting was very influential during the first half of the 19th century. He was a champion of Romantic art which represented uncontrolled nature, including 'human nature' or actions, as opposed to the tradition of classicism which represented fixed ideas of behaviour and standards of beauty. Romanticism was therefore considered 'modern' and attracted modern-thinking artists. Romantic art sometimes looked towards Oriental subject matter which was considered exotic and exciting.

THE STONE-BREAKERS

Gustave Courbet

Courbet believed that artists should only paint '*real and existing things*'. It led to the conclusion that artists should only believe what they could see with their own eyes. This meant painting the people and scenes they could see around them exactly as they appeared, not how they were taught to imagine they should be. Ordinary people in modern dress became the subject matter, and light and its impression on the scene became important. What better way to get closer to the 'truth' than to take the easel and painting to the subject rather than bring the subject to the studio?

WOMAN OF ALGIERS *(detail)*

In 1870 Renoir painted this portrait of a woman of Algiers, heavily influenced by the oriental style that was fashionable at the time. It owes much to Delacroix's painting of the same subject but Renoir's painting has made the transition from an imaginary scene to a very real one. Delacroix's paintings were dominated by Romantic notions of exoticism relying on imaginary far away places. Renoir's *Woman of Algiers*, dressed in an exotic and colourful costume, is depicted as a very real woman. The model was actually Renoir's 19-year-old girlfriend Lise Trehot who directly engages the viewer's gaze in a very sensual way. By placing her in an Oriental costume rather than contemporary French dress, Renoir does not offend his viewer's idea of how women should behave.

INFLUENCES & EARLY WORKS:
IMPRESSIONISM

Renoir's fellow pupils at Charles Gleyre's studio, Monet, Bazille and Sisley, all continued to work together after Gleyre's retirement in 1864. Monet persuaded them to travel to Fontainebleau to paint directly from nature. Renoir's first submission to the official Paris Salon annual exhibition of painting in 1864 was entitled *Esmeralda Dancing with a Goat*. The acceptance of the picture suggests that it was painted in a more traditional style, as the work of the Realists and Impressionists were continually rejected by the Salon. No record exists of this painting because Renoir later destroyed it on the grounds that it contained asphalt and would not last, although possibly it was because he was not content with the way it appeared. Renoir and his fellow painters had set about painting the world around them – the Paris street scenes, local bathing spots, boating on the river Seine and scenes from the cafés and music halls. In 1874 the Société Anonyme des Artistes formed to exhibit their pictures, independent from the official Salon. The first exhibition contained works by Monet, Morisot, Renoir, Degas, Cézanne, Pissarro and Sisley; this group became known as the Impressionists.

THE POPPY FIELD AT ARGENTEUIL

Claude Monet

This picture was painted by Monet in 1873, the year before the first Impressionist exhibition. It shows two pairs of figures walking through a poppy field near his home at Argenteuil on a warm summer's day and has become one of Impressionism's best-known images. Renoir visited Monet at Argenteuil and they went out into the surrounding countryside to paint. Monet and Renoir shared lodgings together when they were young and poor. Renoir later explained that they spent all their money on studio rent, models and coal for the stove to keep the models warm. They would time their cooking with their painting so the hot stove both warmed the models and cooked the food.

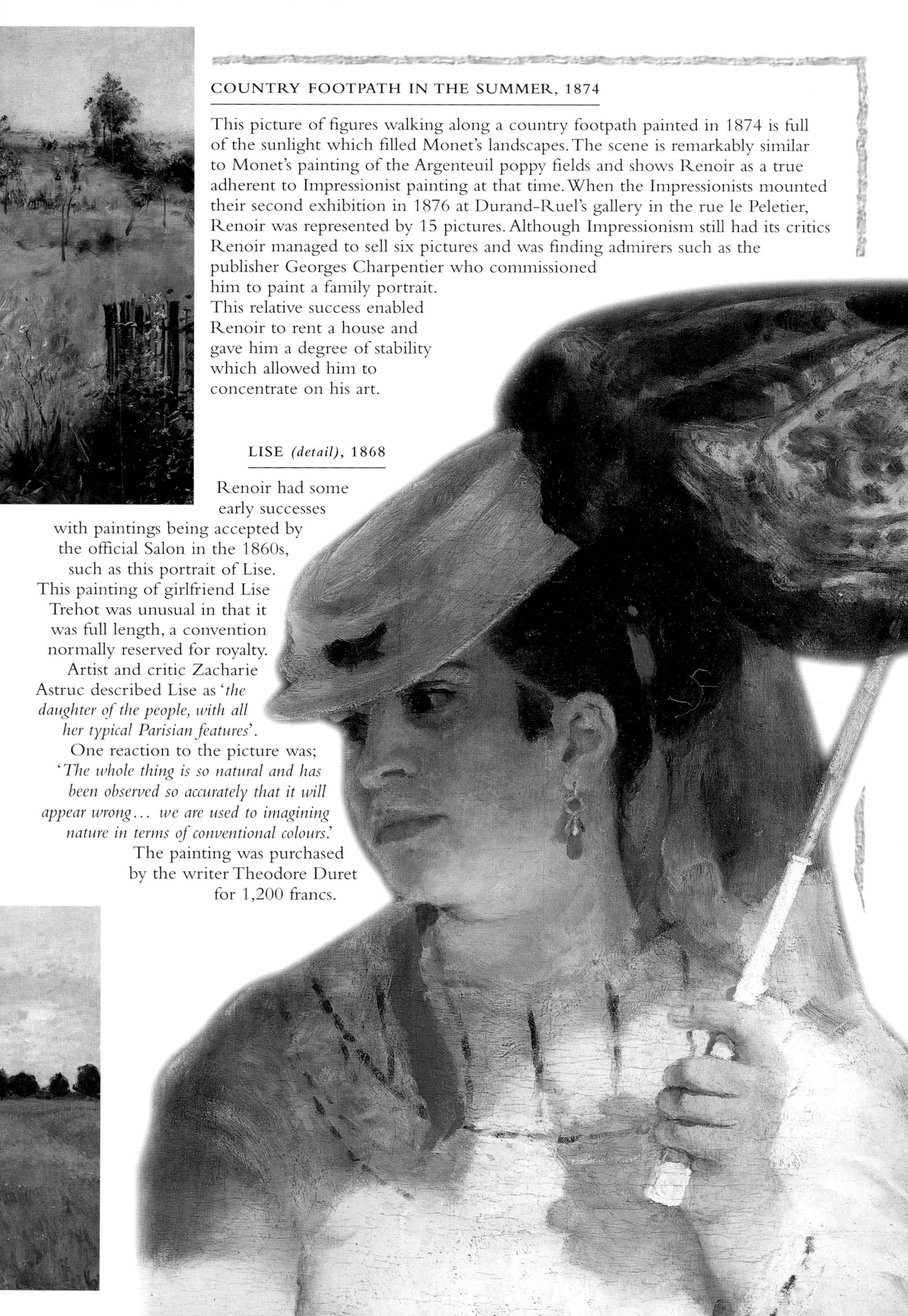

COUNTRY FOOTPATH IN THE SUMMER, 1874

This picture of figures walking along a country footpath painted in 1874 is full of the sunlight which filled Monet's landscapes. The scene is remarkably similar to Monet's painting of the Argenteuil poppy fields and shows Renoir as a true adherent to Impressionist painting at that time. When the Impressionists mounted their second exhibition in 1876 at Durand-Ruel's gallery in the rue le Peletier, Renoir was represented by 15 pictures. Although Impressionism still had its critics Renoir managed to sell six pictures and was finding admirers such as the publisher Georges Charpentier who commissioned him to paint a family portrait. This relative success enabled Renoir to rent a house and gave him a degree of stability which allowed him to concentrate on his art.

LISE *(detail)*, 1868

Renoir had some early successes with paintings being accepted by the official Salon in the 1860s, such as this portrait of Lise. This painting of girlfriend Lise Trehot was unusual in that it was full length, a convention normally reserved for royalty. Artist and critic Zacharie Astruc described Lise as '*the daughter of the people, with all her typical Parisian features*'. One reaction to the picture was; '*The whole thing is so natural and has been observed so accurately that it will appear wrong… we are used to imagining nature in terms of conventional colours.*' The painting was purchased by the writer Theodore Duret for 1,200 francs.

The Life of Renoir

~1841~
Renoir is born on 25 February.

~1854~
Renoir becomes an apprentice at Levy Brothers, painting plates and vases.

~1864~
Has a painting accepted by the Salon but later destroys it.

~1865~
Meets Lise Trehot.

~1872~
Has two paintings purchased by dealer Durand-Ruel and spends the summer painting with Monet.

~1874~
Exhibits at the first Impressionist show.

~1880~
Meets Aline Charigot.

~1883~
Experiments with new 'Dry Style' of painting.

~1885~
Birth of his son Pierre.

~1888~
First attack of rheumatoid arthritis which leaves his face partially paralyzed.

~1892~
Young Girls at the Piano purchased by the State.

~1894~
Birth of son Jean.

~1901~
Birth of son Claude (Coco).

GABRIELLE ET JEAN *(detail)*, C.1895

Renoir's second son, Jean, was born on 15 September 1894. In Jean Renoir's own memoirs of his father he writes that his mother exclaimed on his birth; '*Heavens how ugly, take it away!*' Jean became a famous film director as well as a writer of several books, including a biography of his father. Another witness to Jean's birth was Gabrielle Renard, the 15-year-old cousin of Aline Charigot who had come from her home in Essoyes to help with the preparations for the birth. Gabrielle stayed to help look after Jean. She became Renoir's favourite model, at first posing with the children, as in this portrait with Jean. In Renoir's later years she became an important figure in Renoir's exploration of the female form in such paintings as *Gabrielle with Jewel Box*. Gabrielle continued as Renoir's principal model until 1914 when she married and left the Renoir home in Cagnes.

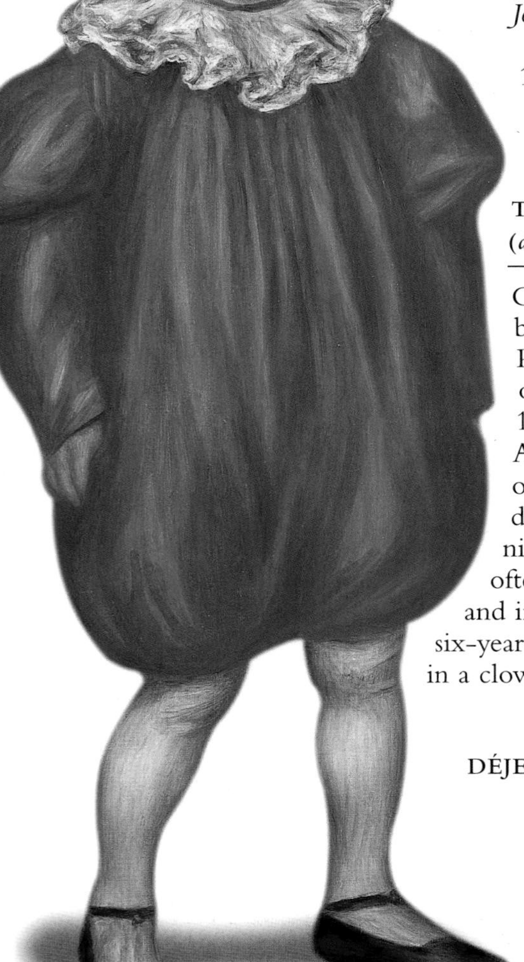

THE CLOWN *(detail)*, 1909

Claude Renoir was born in 1901 when Renoir was 60 years old. Claude was only 14 when his mother, Aline, died at the age of 56, after fighting diabetes. Claude, nicknamed Coco, was often a model for Renoir and in this painting the six-year-old Claude is dressed in a clown's outfit.

DÉJEUNER A BERNEVAL, C.1905

This is a charming domestic interior scene, at home with the Renoir family.

FAMILY, FRIENDS & OTHERS

Renoir did not come from a comfortable middle class family, as many of his Impressionist friends did. His father's tailoring business was just sufficient to support the family and Renoir found a job as an apprentice to a porcelain painter when he was 13 to supplement the family income. When he decided to study painting at the studio of Charles Gleyre he soon became friends with Claude Monet, Frédéric Bazille and Alfred Sisley. He kept company with this artistic circle and had many girlfriends among the models who posed for his paintings, but it was not until Renoir was nearly 40 that he met Aline Charigot, a 19-year-old dressmaker who lived nearby Renoir's home in the rue Saint-Georges. Aline posed for Renoir and fell in love with him despite her mother's advice to find a man who was old and wealthy. Aline travelled to Italy with Renoir in 1881 and much later referred to the trip as their 'honeymoon', despite the fact they were not actually married until 1890.

BUST OF MADAME RENOIR WITH PIERRE

Aline Charigot came from the Burgundy area of France and was teased by her Parisian friends about her accent and country ways. When they first met, Renoir and Aline spent much of their time together by the river Seine, travelling by train from Saint-Lazare to the Chatou bridge and then the Fournaise restaurant. Renoir's well known painting *Luncheon of the Boating Party* (pages 50–51) depicts a scene at the Fournaise restaurant which shows Aline holding a small dog. Aline moved in with Renoir after his return from a trip to Algeria in 1881. Their first child, Pierre, was born in 1885. Renoir found a studio near the family apartments in the rue Houdon in order that, according to Aline, '*the baby will be able to cry to his heart's content.*' Pierre became an actor but went to fight in the First World War where he was badly wounded.

The Life of Renoir

~1905~

Settles in Cagnes-sur-mer on the Mediterranean coast.

~1911~

Confined to a wheelchair but continues to paint with brushes tied to his hands.

~1915~

Aline dies at the age of 56.

~1919~

Visits the Louvre to see his paintings hanging with the old masters.

Dies on 3 December.

FAMILY, FRIENDS & OTHERS

The small group of friends who studied together under Charles Gleyre and then continued to paint together were at the very centre of the movement which was subsequently named Impressionism. In 1865 Renoir shared a studio with Alfred Sisley and a year later, after Sisley was married, he moved in with Frédéric Bazille, a talented young painter who was tragically killed at the age of 29 during the Franco-Prussian war. In 1867 Bazille rented a Paris studio at 20 rue Visconti. From here he wrote to his mother; *'Since my last letter there is something new at the rue Visconti. Monet has fallen from the sky with a collection of huge canvases which will be a great success at the World Fair. He will stay here until the end of the month. With Renoir that makes two needy painters that I'm housing. It's a veritable sanatorium. I'm delighted, I have plenty of space, and both are very good company.'* Renoir and Bazille continued to be close friends, later moving together to a studio near the famous Café Guerbois which became the meeting place for the new wave of modern-thinking artists such as Manet, Monet, Degas, and Pissarro, as well as writers like Émile Zola, Edmond Duranty and Zacharie Astruc.

PORTRAIT OF JULIE MANET *(detail)*, *c.*1894

Julie Manet often stayed with the Renoir family, particularly after the death of her parents, Berthe Morisot and Eugène Manet, which left her orphaned at the age of 17. Morisot had asked Renoir to look after Julie although her official guardian was the poet Stéphane Mallarmé.

MADAME ALPHONSE DAUDET *(detail)*, 1875

Alphonse Daudet was a successful novelist and playwright who, together with such writers as Émile Zola, was regarded as one of the leading members of the Realist movement in literature. Daudet was a great supporter of Impressionism, commissioning this portrait of his wife and buying works from a number of other artists. He was a frequent visitor to the Nouvelle-Athènes café, mixing with the artistic set who met to talk about their work. He was also often invited to Renoir's house where he would join the likes of Zola, Odilon Redon and Stéphane Mallarmé for dinner.

PORTRAIT OF CLAUDE MONET *(detail)*, 1875

Claude Monet moved to Argenteuil, a suburb of Paris, in 1871. Renoir was amongst the many visitors that stayed with Monet at Argenteuil. When they were together Monet persuaded Renoir to take up his easel and go out into the countryside to paint, *en plein-air*. Several of Renoir's paintings are of views of the Seine such as the picture of racing boats entitled *The Seine at Argenteuil*. Renoir also made numerous portraits of his friend Claude Monet and Claude's wife Camille. Monet's obsession with capturing in paint the changing moods of his subject matter according to the light made him the leading exponent of Impressionism. In his own words, Monet wanted to *'ensnare the light, and throw it directly on to the canvas'*.

PORTRAIT OF RICHARD WAGNER, 1882

Renoir was introduced to Wagner's music by a friend at a time when national sentiment was against the composer. This made Renoir determined to like his music and Renoir was eventually introduced to Wagner in person, at which time he made three sketches, (executed in under an hour) and this portrait. During the meeting Wagner managed to offend the artist because of his views of French composers whom Wagner hated. Renoir expressed his like for the music of Offenbach which Wagner dismissed as *'little music, but not bad'*. Later on Renoir attended a performance of Wagner's opéra *Die Walküre* at Bayreuth, and commented; *'They have no right to shut people up in the dark for three solid hours… you are forced to look at the only place where there is any light; the stage. It's absolute tyranny… We might as well be frank about it; Wagner's music is boring.'*

LE MOULIN DE LA GALETTE, 1876

The painting, which has been described as the most beautiful picture of the 19th century, appears at first glance to be chaotic. The foreground and background merge and the overlapping forms of the figures are often indistinguishable. The sunlight that filters through the foliage casts shadows that fall across the figures and ground alike, creating a dappled effect that unifies the picture.

Renoir made many studies from models for his figures in *Le Moulin de la Galette.* The two young girls in the centre of the picture, one resting her arm on the other's shoulder, are Jeanne and Estelle, seamstresses known as 'grisettes,' dressed in the latest Paris style. Renoir described how he saw Jeanne on the streets of Montmartre, thought her the ideal model, and stopped and spoke to her. *'I don't go in for that sort of thing Monsieur,'* she replied. Renoir noted that; *'She had lovely hands, the ends of her fingers were swollen from being pricked by needles.'* Eventually Renoir persuaded Jeanne's mother to let her daughter pose for him in return for payment, and soon Jeanne's sister Estelle also became Renoir's model.

The pair of dancers depicted centre-left is the Cuban painter Pedro Vidal with Margot Legrand. Margot appears to be the same young girl who Jean Renoir recalls was nursed by his father and Dr Gachet, but she died of suspected small-pox three years after this picture was painted.

WHAT DO RENOIR'S PAINTINGS SAY?

PARIS SOCIETY

The years before the end of the 19th century are known in France as the Belle Époque, the golden age when life was for the enjoying. This description does not convey the fact that it was also the time when many were struggling for equal rights such as workers and women in general. Nevertheless it was a time when Paris prospered with new roads, railways and buildings and the middle classes became more secure and prosperous. Mass entertainment was available in the form of the café-concerts and dance halls, the most popular of which was the *Folies-Bergère* which still exists today. Renoir painted modern Parisian life; images of young people at play, in the park, the dance hall, strolling along the boulevards show us the pleasant side of Paris life. Renoir was aware that he concentrated on the nice things when he said *'There are enough unpleasant things in this world. We don't have to paint them as well.'* Although Renoir concentrated on the pleasant side of life he painted scenes from the ordinary everyday world of the Parisian worker at play, not the fashionable well-to-do classes, and it is this record of real life that makes his painting fascinating.

The pipe smoker (on the left) is Norbert Goeneutte and seated next to him with pen poised is writer Georges Rivière.

DANCING AT THE MOULIN DE LA GALETTE

A building programme in the 1860s and 1870s transformed the landscape of Paris. Some of the surrounding parishes became part of the city as it grew and grew. Montmartre had been a village on a hill with windmills and vineyards, before it was swallowed up by Paris. The fashion for public dances in the 1870s meant that nearly every available space in Paris, from bars and courtyards to squares and parks, were at some time used for this new craze. The best-known dance-bar in Montmartre was le Moulin de la Galette, or 'le Radet' for short. It had an outdoor dance floor as well as a bar for red wine and 'galettes', a kind of circular waffle from which it gained its name.

FAMOUS IMAGES

By the end of the 1870s Renoir was no longer exhibiting with the Impressionists and had decided to follow his own individual course. When he painted the *Luncheon of the Boating Party* in 1881 he had already made a break with Impressionism. He stated that *'I had wrung Impressionism dry, and I finally came to the conclusion that I neither knew how to paint nor draw. In a word, Impressionism was a blind alley.'* His tours of Algeria and then Italy gave him new inspiration and new direction, and he rediscovered the works of the Old Masters. The style employed in the execution of the *Luncheon of the Boating Party* is more assured than that of *Le Moulin de la Galette* painted five years earlier. The individual figures portrayed are more clearly defined, particularly by the use of stronger colour, and the forms appear to be gaining greater solidity.

YOUNG WOMAN WITH A FAN (*detail*), 1881

This portrait of Alphonsine, daughter of restaurant owner Alphonse Fournaise, captures the charm which made her a favoured model with many male admirers. She features in *Luncheon of the Boating Party*, leaning against the rail.

LUNCHEON OF THE BOATING PARTY, 1880/1

The scene depicted in this well-known painting is the Restaurant Fournaise on the Ile de Chatou, a little island in the River Seine near the Ile de Croissy. It was a short train ride from Renoir's studio in the centre of Paris. The owner of the restaurant, Alphonse Fournaise, had built a landing stage for the Parisians who wished to swim and hire boats on the river, and he began to serve refreshments on the stage. Renoir recalls the place *'where life was a perpetual holiday and the world knew how to laugh in those days.'* Renoir often used to visit the Restaurant Fournaise with his girlfriend Aline.

The figure wearing a top hat and engaged in conversation at the back of the scene is the banker and art collector Charles Ephrussi.

Aline Charigot, Renoir's future wife, sits at the table holding a small dog. Behind is Alphonse Fournaise, the restaurant owner.

In the background is Paul Lhote holding actress Jeanne Samary by the waist.

The seated figure wearing the straw hat is painter Gustave Caillebotte who talks to actress Ellen Andrée.

RENOIR'S FRIENDS

The painting shows many of Renoir's friends, several of whom sat for Renoir in his studio so he could finish the picture. The group is notable for its social mix, with flower sellers and bankers drinking side by side. The relaxed scene is full of meaningful glances and intimate touches.

THE UMBRELLAS, 1881-6

This painting clearly demonstrates Renoir's different approaches to painting in the 1880s. The artist returned to this painting again and again over a period of years. The figures on the right of the picture are painted in Renoir's 'Impressionist' style of the 1870s with bright colours but soft outlines and loose brushstrokes. The two figures on the left however were painted in a later style which has more clearly defined outlines, a more 'finished' surface and more subdued colours.

It is thought that the painting was begun around 1881 because the right-hand figures are wearing dresses and hats that were fashionable at that time, and Renoir normally dressed his models in the latest fashions. By 1883 simpler dresses came into style and the woman holding a basket is dressed in a style which was the height of fashion in 1885, but which had fallen out of fashion by 1887. Recent X-ray examination of the painting suggests that the woman on the left was first painted in the earlier Impressionist method around 1881 with skirts similar to the other women in the picture, complete with white lace cuffs and collar and a hat. This figure was over-painted in about 1885.

DETECTION THROUGH COLOUR

Further examination of *The Umbrellas* reveals the presence of cobalt blue pigment in the right hand section of the picture and in the original painting underneath the left-hand figures. This pigment was used by Renoir only during the 1870s and early 1880s. French Ultramarine, a pigment used later by Renoir, was found in the colours on the left-hand figures we see today. He also experimented with removing the oil medium and replacing it with a water-based medium to bind the colours because he thought the oil would eventually darken and spoil his colours, although this experiment was without success. This examination of the use of pigments and medium enables art historians to find out the history of the painting.

HOW WERE THE PAINTINGS MADE?

THE DRY STYLE

When Renoir visited Italy in 1881 he went to see the art of the great masters such as Michelangelo, Raphael and Bernini. He later recalled that he became tired of the draped figures with too many folds and muscles, and preferred the Pompeiian frescoes in the Naples Museum. He marvelled at the wonderful colours achieved by the fresco painters with such a limited range of colours made from earths and vegetable dyes, and even confessed to repairing a wall painting using paints in powder form that he found in a nearby mason's house. The experience of Renoir's Italian trip was certainly one factor that made him change the way he was painting. By 1883 Renoir openly admitted that Impressionism was a dead end and that he was looking for a new style. He rejected the Impressionist way of painting outdoors, stating that *'An artist who paints straight from nature is really only looking for nothing but momentary effects. He does not try to be creative himself, and as a result the pictures soon become monotonous.'* Renoir's exploration of new ways of painting in the 1880s have now become known as his 'Dry Period'.

THE SCHOOL OF ATHENS *(detail)*

Raphael

Renoir's gradual disillusionment with the Impressionist style of rapidly building-up the surface of the canvas with touches of colour was hastened by what he saw on his trip to Italy. He admired the purity and grandeur of Raphael's wall paintings which retained bright colourful surfaces and were masterful compositions with great clarity of structure and form.

WHAT DO RENOIR'S PAINTINGS SAY?

A NEW DIRECTION

Renoir's 'Dry Period' is also sometimes known as his 'Ingresque Period' after the famous French painter Jean Ingres. Ingres was a dominant influence in French painting in the earlier part of the 19th century. Ingres spent a good part of his career in Italy and was a devoted follower of the art of Raphael, the great Italian painter of the High Renaissance. The art of Ingres, in his admiration of Raphael, was in turn admired by Renoir. This direct line of influence extends back to Raphael's source of inspiration; the great classical art of ancient Greece. In pursuing this new direction in his painting Renoir was rejecting the modern art of Impressionism which he felt had lost its way. He was returning to the traditional values which had remained unchanged for centuries. Renoir became interested in the methods of Renaissance artists and he criticized the modern teaching methods which had replaced the apprenticeship system. The culmination of his new direction was a large painting called *The Bathers*.

THE BLONDE BATHER

This painting was made by Renoir in 1887 at the height of his 'Dry Period'. The influence of Ingres is quite evident, the formal pose of the figure against a classical landscape recalling the fresco paintings Renoir had visited during his trip to Italy. The painting resembles fresco painting because of its bright colouring, smooth finish and clear edges around the female form. However Renoir does not resist breaking-up the landscape with individually applied brushstrokes. About this time a critic asked Renoir whether he considered himself a descendant of Ingres, to which Renoir replied *'I only wish I was.'*

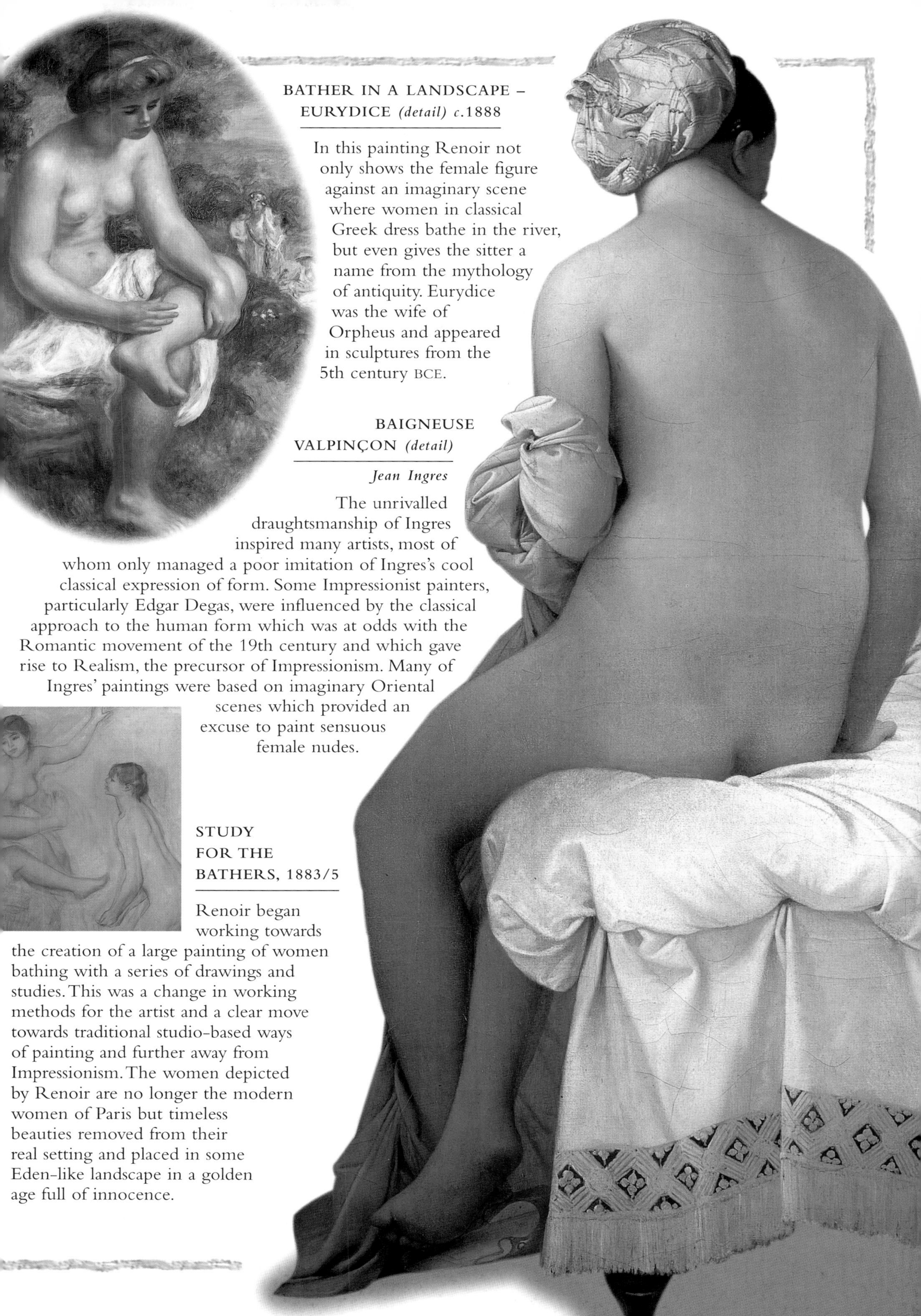

BATHER IN A LANDSCAPE – EURYDICE *(detail)* *c.*1888

In this painting Renoir not only shows the female figure against an imaginary scene where women in classical Greek dress bathe in the river, but even gives the sitter a name from the mythology of antiquity. Eurydice was the wife of Orpheus and appeared in sculptures from the 5th century BCE.

BAIGNEUSE VALPINÇON *(detail)*

Jean Ingres

The unrivalled draughtsmanship of Ingres inspired many artists, most of whom only managed a poor imitation of Ingres's cool classical expression of form. Some Impressionist painters, particularly Edgar Degas, were influenced by the classical approach to the human form which was at odds with the Romantic movement of the 19th century and which gave rise to Realism, the precursor of Impressionism. Many of Ingres' paintings were based on imaginary Oriental scenes which provided an excuse to paint sensuous female nudes.

STUDY FOR THE BATHERS, 1883/5

Renoir began working towards the creation of a large painting of women bathing with a series of drawings and studies. This was a change in working methods for the artist and a clear move towards traditional studio-based ways of painting and further away from Impressionism. The women depicted by Renoir are no longer the modern women of Paris but timeless beauties removed from their real setting and placed in some Eden-like landscape in a golden age full of innocence.

THE GREAT BATHERS –
THE NYMPHS *(detail)*

Renoir continued the theme of Bathers from the 1880s to the end of his life. This picture was painted about 1918, when Renoir was 77 years old. The figures in the pastoral landscape appear almost to be part of the ground upon which they lie. They have a massiveness and solidity which makes them appear like sculptures modelled out of clay, but are painted in striking flesh tones which are echoed in the grass and the trees which surround them. Renoir was racked by arthritis towards the end of his life and was only able to paint by having his paintbrushes wedged into his bandaged hands. It was in this way that the *The Great Bathers* was painted.

THE BATHERS

Renoir exhibited his new paintings at the Georges Petit Gallery. They were exhibited alongside paintings by artists such as Monet, Pissarro, Morisot and Whistler, and caused something of a stir because of Renoir's departure from Impressionism. The painter Camille Pissarro, a friend of Renoir, wrote to his son; *'Durand has been to Petits; he has seen the Renoirs, and doesn't like his new style – he doesn't like it at all.'* Durand-Ruel was an influential dealer who had championed Impressionist art and he was evidently discouraged to find that one of his artists had now adopted a different style of painting. Pissarro commented on Renoir's new style; *'I can quite understand the effort he is making. It is a very good thing not to want to go on repeating oneself, but he has concentrated all his effort on line. The figures stand out against each other without any sort of relationship and the whole thing is meaningless. Renoir is no draughtsman and without the lovely colours he used to use he is incoherent.'*

NYMPHS BATHING *François Girardon*

This bas-relief of nymphs bathing by the 17th-century artist François Girardon decorates one of the fountain pools in the park of Versailles. Renoir found it a source of inspiration for his *Bathers* picture as well as other works.

THE BATHERS

This painting was made over a period of several years and finally exhibited at Georges Petit's gallery in 1887. Renoir has created a picture which is completely unlike his former Impressionist works. The subject matter is drawn from a classical source and has none of the spontaneity in execution that typifies Impressionism. In fact the pigment was spread with a knife and smoothed over as much as possible to create a highly finished surface. The idealized beauty of the female forms in their carefully arranged poses have nothing to do with Paris in the 1880s and are divorced from any real or natural context. The women recall the porcelain decorations that Renoir made in his youth and the only real similarity with his earlier painting is the richness of colour, particularly in the surrounding landscape, which typifies Renoir's art.

DIANA BATHING

François Boucher

The Rococo style of the 18th-century artist François Boucher was much admired by Renoir. Boucher's paintings of beautiful young women in classical landscapes were an obvious inspiration, as much for the subject matter as the style of painting.

GABRIELLE WITH JEWEL BOX, 1910

This painting made in 1910 shows Renoir's late style. The model is Gabrielle Renard, the young cousin of Renoir's wife Aline. Renoir was quite open about his fascination for women's bodies and talked about them in a way some would find unacceptable today. To the artist they were objects to be observed and depicted: the quality of the skin compared to a fruit which must respond well to the light; the arrangement of the facial features must be in harmony *'with almond shaped eyes which should be half-way between the top of the head and the tip of the chin.'* Some critics think that this is why his models appear to be without spirit – they are painted as if they were fruit or flowers. Renoir's depiction of the female form is without lust. The women appear trance-like, increasingly detached from their surroundings.

BATHER WITH LONG HAIR (*detail*), 1910

Renoir concentrated on voluptuous nudes who posed in a sea of vibrant colour, and it is almost as if his struggle with arthritis which gave him difficulty holding his paintbrushes allowed him the artistic freedom to relax his style, painting in a freer way with looser, broader brushstrokes. The female figures are as one with the landscape, and no longer appear to be conscious compositions, carefully arranged, but merge effortlessly with the background creating natural and sensuous imagery.

HOW WERE THE PAINTINGS MADE?

THE LATE STYLE

In the 1890s Impressionist painting was becoming established in some circles, particularly with some influential collectors, but as a style of painting it was being surpassed by new styles such as the Symbolism of Paul Gauguin. Renoir by this time was an old man who suffered severe attacks of crippling rheumatoid arthritis which forced him to spend the winter months in the relative warmth of the South of France. Finally in 1905 he moved with his family to Cagnes, a small town near Antibes on the Mediterranean coast. He had a house built which he called 'Les Collettes' which was to become his studio until his death. Towards the end of his life his arthritis was so severe that he was permanently wheelchair-bound and his hands became deformed to such an extent that he was unable to hold any object. He continued to paint with brushes wedged into his bandaged hands, and his pictures became more colourful than ever before.

THE JUDGEMENT OF PARIS

Peter Paul Rubens

Renoir's depiction of the female form developed and became more massive, taking on proportions which remind us of the 17th-century Dutch artist Rubens, and dominate the picture frame. The figures are completely timeless and might be from classical mythology or from the present day, but are isolated from everything except their landscape. The backgrounds are reduced to a field of colour, still Impressionistic in execution, and the whole is soaked in the Mediterranean sunlight which make the colours come alive.

CATHERINE HESSLING IN THE FILM NANA (*right*)

Catherine Hessling (also shown with Renoir in his studio) was a model who worked at the Nice Académie de Peinture and who went to work for Renoir when he was looking for models for his large *Great Bathers* painting. Dédée, as she was then known, travelled by train every day from Nice to Renoir's studio in Cagnes to pose for the artist. After Renoir's death in 1919 his son Jean married Dédée and she became an actress appearing in the early films directed by Jean Renoir, under her stage name Catherine Hessling.

THE AUDIENCE FOR RENOIR'S PICTURES

Renoir had no means of financial support except from odd jobs or from the sale of his paintings. At the beginning of his career as an artist, times were hard. The society formed by the Impressionist group in 1873, with Renoir a member, had to be dissolved in 1875 due to large debts and the artists were forced to sell their pictures. They were auctioned at the Hotel Drouot in Paris on 24 March 1875 with disastrous results. With a hostile crowd and few buyers, Renoir sold 20 canvases for 2,000 francs compared to the 200,000 francs a respected Salon artist could earn for one painting alone. Early on, Renoir depended on friends to purchase paintings, receiving support from Édouard Manet, Victor Chocquet and others. Chocquet was a civil servant in the Ministry of Finance who could ill afford to buy paintings. Renoir is reported to have said of him: '*What a charming crackpot... he scraped up the means to buy paintings from his salary... and never gave a thought to whether or not the art would appreciate in value.*'

PORTRAIT OF DELPHINE LEGRAND *(detail)*, 1878

Some of the most charming of all Renoir's work are his portraits of children. In this picture of Delphine Legrand, daughter of friend and art dealer Alphonse Legrand, Renoir is able to create a sense of innocence and vulnerability which captures the spirit of the sitter.

MONSIEUR AND MADAME BERNHEIM, 1910

The Bernheim family were art dealers who actively supported the Impressionist painters. The Bernheims organized an important exhibition for Renoir in 1900 and continued to represent his work up to and beyond Renoir's death. During this time Renoir made several portraits of the Bernheim family members including this picture of Benheim-Jeune and his wife. The family was very rich, with a magnificent château, a house in Paris, a dozen motorcars, and even an airship. Most importantly to Renoir, however, was that they had '*beautiful wives whose skins took to the light.*'

MADAME CHARPENTIER *(detail)*

In 1876 Renoir painted this portrait of Marguerite Charpentier, wife of Georges Charpentier, the publisher of famous novelists such as Flaubert, Zola and Maupassant. The family were very wealthy and had a reputation for gathering together the most interesting people of the day; writers, painters, composers, as well as actresses and popular singers. The Charpentiers supported Renoir as they did other artists, commissioning portraits of the family and using their influence to ensure his paintings were exhibited, thereby giving Renoir a degree of financial security. Renoir noted of the sessions with Marguerite Charpentier; '*She reminds me of the sweethearts of my youth, the models of Fragonard. The two daughters had lovely dimples. I was congratulated. I forgot the attacks of the newspapers. I had models who were willing to sit for free and who were full of goodwill.*'

PINK AND BLUE, 1881

Alice and Elizabeth Cahen d'Anvers were daughters of a wealthy banker. Renoir was commissioned to paint several portraits of the two girls after Charles Ephrussi, owner of the *Gazette des Beaux-Arts* had introduced Renoir to the Cahen family. It appears that the Cahens were disappointed with the double portrait and decided to hang it in the servants quarters, out of view of their friends.

WHAT THE CRITICS SAY

Renoir's art has justifiably taken its place among the great Impressionist works and he is considered today to be one of the small group who changed the course of art in the latter half of the 19th century. Like his contemporary painters he found acceptance slow during his working life, but towards the end of his career gained recognition, fame and the money that came with it. Renoir never had any pretensions about his art; he wanted to paint what he found attractive and amusing, and by his own admission did not dwell on any concern to express great ideas or emotions. He hated any notion of artists being more than simple labourers who day after day had a job to do – paint. This may be because of his relatively humble beginnings, but whatever the reason critics, and especially art historians, in the 20th century have regarded his art as somehow slighter, less important than his contemporaries. By contrast the non-specialist public at large have always found his art attractive, accessible and enjoyable.

NUDE IN THE SUNLIGHT, 1876

In 1876 Durand-Ruel exhibited Renoir's paintings at the rue le Pelletier, including *Nude in the Sunlight*. The art critic Albert Wolff wrote in *Le Figaro; 'Try and explain to Monsieur Renoir that a woman's torso is not a mass of rotting flesh, with violet-toned green spots all over it, indicating a corpse in the final stages of decay… And this collection of vulgarities has been exhibited in public without a thought for possible fatal consequences. Only yesterday a poor man was arrested in the rue le Pelletier, after leaving the exhibition, because he began biting everyone in sight.'*

PORTRAIT OF A YOUNG GIRL *(detail)*, 1888

Renoir's habit of making the eyes of his portrait subjects dark in contrast to the surrounding pale face attracted the attention of Arthur Baignieres, who wrote of Renoir's painting *Mother and Children* in 1874; *'From afar we see a bluish haze, from which six chocolate drops forcefully emerge. Whatever could it be? We come closer; the sweets are the eyes of three people and the haze a mother and her daughters.'*

YOUNG GIRLS AT THE PIANO, 1892

In 1892 the poet Stéphane Mallarmé and the art critic Claude Roger-Marx persuaded Henri Roujon, the Director of the Beaux-Arts, to purchase a Renoir painting for the State collection. An informal commission resulted in Renoir painting five versions of *Young Girls at the Piano*. The State purchased one of the pictures on 2 May 1892 for the sum of 4,000 francs. The State had only acquired paintings by one other of the original Impressionist group, Alfred Sisley. Mallarmé stated his support for Renoir in a letter to Roujon: *'It is my feeling, as well as the agreed opinion of everyone else, that you cannot be sufficiently congratulated on having chosen such a definitive, refreshing, bold work of maturity for a museum.'* Two years earlier Renoir's friends had asked on his behalf for him to be decorated by the State for his work as a painter, but Renoir refused the honour.

NEWS OF THE DIFFERENT EXHIBITIONS

There is an exhibition of the INTRANSIGENTS (Impressionists) in the Boulevard des Capucines, or rather, you might say, of the LUNATICS, of which I have already given you a report. If you would like to be amused, and have a little time to spare, don't miss it.

At the time of the first Impressionist exhibitions the press were very hostile. This article is from the paper *La Patrie* on 14 May 1874.

DEGAS

BELLELLI FAMILY, 1858/9

In 1856 Degas travelled to Italy, staying at his grandfather's splendid villa in San Rocco di Capodimonte. He spent the following two years touring the country, stopping in Rome for a period to study at the Academie. He had many relations in Italy, several of whose portraits he painted whilst visiting. Degas painted this portrait of his aunt Laura's family, the Bellellis, on his return to Paris. The portrait is a masterpiece which captures not just the likenesses, but the mood and tension of a proud family who are in mourning for Laura's recently dead father. Degas was happy during his spell in Italy: he was amongst family, spoke fluent Italian, and most of all was free to study the art and architecture of the Italian Renaissance.

THE OPERA HOUSE AT PLACE DE L'OPÉRA

Degas was a great lover of the opera, and during one of his rare periods away from Paris had written '*the lack of an Opera is a real privation*'. The Opera House frequented by Degas, and which stands in the Place de l'Opéra today, was opened in 1875 after the Opera House in the rue le Peletier burnt to the ground.

DEGAS' PARIS

Degas lived all his life in Paris. He exhibited paintings with his fellow artists but never considered himself an Impressionist painter. He was an avid art collector, and devoted more time to collecting than painting as the onset of blindness gradually curtailed his work. By 1908 he had more or less given up painting and lived a sad existence until his death in 1917. During the final years of his life, he shuffled along the streets of Paris feeling his way with his cane, oblivious to the new sounds of motor cars rushing past, repeating again and again, '*Death is all I think of.*'

SELF-PORTRAIT OF DEGAS AS A YOUNG MAN, 1855

Degas was fortunate to belong to a wealthy family and could therefore indulge his passion for art, supported by his father. In 1859, at the age of 25, Degas had his own studio in the rue Madame in Paris although he continued to live in his father's house. He soon began to mix with the other artists who made up the café society in Paris at that time, and who were to be instrumental in changing the course of art in the 19th century. The focus in the 1860s was the Café Guerbois in the Batignolles district, where Édouard Manet was the best-known figure. Manet and Degas were to have a strong influence on each other.

THE WORLD OF DEGAS

Edgar Degas was born in Paris on 19 July 1834. His father, Auguste, had only recently moved to Paris from Naples, coming from a wealthy banking family. Auguste chose to change the spelling of the family name from Degas to 'de Gas' to make it appear as if he came from a noble background. In Paris Auguste met and married an American girl called Celestine Musson. Edgar was their first child. Auguste de Gas was a banker by trade but was very interested in the arts, particularly music and the theatre, and encouraged the young Edgar's artistic interests. Although Edgar enrolled in Law School, he soon abandoned his studies in favour of painting. In 1855 he began attending the École des Beaux-Arts to learn painting, but spent most of his time visiting relatives in Florence and Naples where he studied the works of the great Italian masters. His own work, developed on the belief that drawing was the foundation of good painting, was to match the techniques of the great Renaissance artists such as Leonardo da Vinci and Michelangelo.

Detail of a self-portrait c.1857-60

INFLUENCES & EARLY WORKS

Degas was impressed by the art of the great French and Italian masters and devoted himself to copying their works in order to learn their craft. When he visited Rome in 1857 he filled 28 sketchbooks, drawing obsessively from the art he saw around him, and by 1860 he had copied no fewer than 700 Renaissance and Classical works. In his early career Degas was heavily influenced by Eugène Delacroix and particularly Jean Auguste Dominique Ingres. During his lifetime he acquired 20 paintings and 28 drawings by Ingres as well as works by Delacroix. At first Degas emulated his favourite artists by painting pictures which referred back to the classical school, depicting scenes from ancient Greece, but he soon realized his pictures were out of date and sought new subjects. Realist contemporaries such as the painters Gustave Courbet and Édouard Manet, and the writers Charles Baudelaire and Émile Zola, were convinced that art should reflect real life, rather than romanticized views or themes drawn from classical antiquity. These influences, especially Manet's views, made Degas believe that modern life could be a source of 'heroic' subject matter. Henceforth Degas concentrated on the real world around him.

THE DEATH OF SARDANAPALUS

Eugène Delacroix

Eugène Delacroix was one of the great artists of the first half of the 19th century. His dramatic canvases depicted exotic literary subjects, often stories from north Africa (which he visited in 1832), in direct contrast to the prevailing French classical style of artists such as Ingres. Delacroix's romantic imagery was executed in brilliant colour which made him a favourite of the Impressionist painters who were to follow. Degas was a great admirer of Delacroix, unlike his father, as this excerpt from a letter demonstrates: *'You know that I am far from sharing your opinion of Delacroix, a painter who has abandoned himself to the chaos of his notions and unfortunately for himself has neglected the art of drawing, that keystone on which everything depends.'*

THE SUFFERING OF THE CITY OF NEW ORLEANS, 1865

This painting was the first that Degas had accepted by the French Salon exhibition in 1865. It is not surprising that it received little attention, because Manet's painting of *Olympia* was in the same exhibition and scandalized Paris society. Degas' medieval war scene appeared very old-fashioned when compared with Manet's daring portrayal of a naked Olympia, recognizably a modern-day courtesan. If Degas had intended to comment on the fate of New Orleans, which had been occupied by Union troops in the American Civil War three years earlier, his message had not been made clear.

SEMIRAMIS BUILDING BABYLON

This painting of 1861 is an uneasy combination of the styles of both Delacroix and Ingres. The subject is Semiramis, legendary queen of Assyria and founder of Babylon, who was supposed to have massacred all her slaves after one night of passion. The exotic Oriental story, which would have attracted Delacroix, has been painted in a classical style which borrows from antiquity – quite literally in the case of the horse. The stillness of the scene is reminiscent of Ingres but appears very false and theatrical.

THE EXECUTION OF MAXIMILIAN

Édouard Manet

Manet painted four versions of this painting, showing the execution of the Archduke Maximilian of Austria, who had been installed as Emperor of Mexico by the French after the supression of Benito Juárez's revolutionary republic government. After Maximilian's downfall he was sentenced to death. The sheer brutality of the scene is conveyed in an almost journalistic way by Manet. The second version was cut up by Leon, Manet's son, after the artist's death. Leon considered only a part of the picture good enough to sell (the sergeant examining his rifle – *see left*), which he sold to Degas. Although interest from buyers persuaded Leon to recover and sell other portions of the picture some had gone forever, apparently used by Leon to light a fire.

Self-portrait of the artist (above right) with Evariste de Valernnes, 1865.

The Life of Degas

~1834~
Edgar de Gas is born on 19 July.

~1847~
Celestine de Gas, Edgar's mother, dies.

~1860~
Stays with the Valpinçon family in Normandy.

~1865~
The Suffering of the City of New Orleans is exhibited at the Paris Salon exhibition.

~1872~
Travels to London and then New Orleans.

~1874~
Degas' father dies.

Exhibits his work with the first Impressionist exhibition.

~1878~
Degas' painting *Portrait in a New Orleans Cotton Office* is bought by the Musée des Beaux-Arts.

FAMILY, FRIENDS & OTHERS

Edgar Degas came from a large wealthy banking family which had relations in several countries, including America and Italy. His French grandfather moved to Italy, marrying an Italian named Aurora Freppa. They had seven children including Edgar's father, Auguste. Auguste in turn moved back to Paris in the 1830s where he met and married Celestine Musson, an American girl from New Orleans whose family originated from the French slave-owning population in Saint-Dominique (Haiti). Musson's family had moved to New Orleans after the revolution of Toussaint-Louverture. Auguste Degas and Celestine Musson had four children including Edgar. Celestine died when Edgar was 13 years old. Auguste brought up his children alone, educating them at the finest schools in Paris, cultivating in his children a love of the arts, especially music and painting. He often took Edgar to the Louvre to admire the paintings of the French and Italian masters and had his own collection which included many fine works. In a letter to his son, Auguste wrote; *'Follow... that path which lies before you, which you yourself have laid open. It is yours and yours alone... you can be sure you will achieve great things. You have a splendid career ahead of you, do not be discouraged and do not torment yourself... You speak of boredom in doing portraits, you must overcome this for portraiture will be one of the finest jewels in your crown.'*

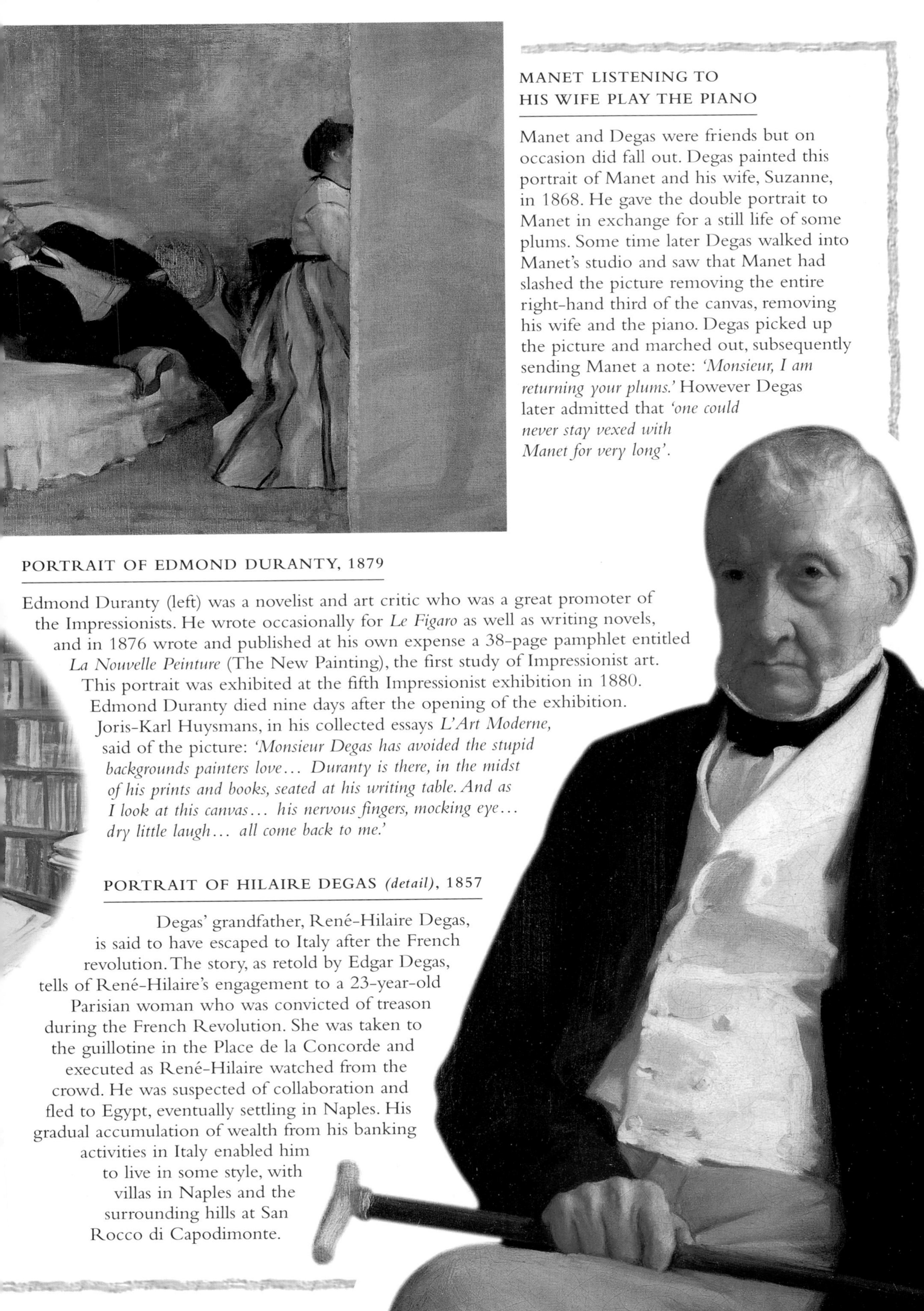

MANET LISTENING TO HIS WIFE PLAY THE PIANO

Manet and Degas were friends but on occasion did fall out. Degas painted this portrait of Manet and his wife, Suzanne, in 1868. He gave the double portrait to Manet in exchange for a still life of some plums. Some time later Degas walked into Manet's studio and saw that Manet had slashed the picture removing the entire right-hand third of the canvas, removing his wife and the piano. Degas picked up the picture and marched out, subsequently sending Manet a note: *'Monsieur, I am returning your plums.'* However Degas later admitted that *'one could never stay vexed with Manet for very long'*.

PORTRAIT OF EDMOND DURANTY, 1879

Edmond Duranty (left) was a novelist and art critic who was a great promoter of the Impressionists. He wrote occasionally for *Le Figaro* as well as writing novels, and in 1876 wrote and published at his own expense a 38-page pamphlet entitled *La Nouvelle Peinture* (The New Painting), the first study of Impressionist art. This portrait was exhibited at the fifth Impressionist exhibition in 1880. Edmond Duranty died nine days after the opening of the exhibition. Joris-Karl Huysmans, in his collected essays *L'Art Moderne,* said of the picture: *'Monsieur Degas has avoided the stupid backgrounds painters love… Duranty is there, in the midst of his prints and books, seated at his writing table. And as I look at this canvas… his nervous fingers, mocking eye… dry little laugh… all come back to me.'*

PORTRAIT OF HILAIRE DEGAS *(detail)*, 1857

Degas' grandfather, René-Hilaire Degas, is said to have escaped to Italy after the French revolution. The story, as retold by Edgar Degas, tells of René-Hilaire's engagement to a 23-year-old Parisian woman who was convicted of treason during the French Revolution. She was taken to the guillotine in the Place de la Concorde and executed as René-Hilaire watched from the crowd. He was suspected of collaboration and fled to Egypt, eventually settling in Naples. His gradual accumulation of wealth from his banking activities in Italy enabled him to live in some style, with villas in Naples and the surrounding hills at San Rocco di Capodimonte.

HORTENSE VALPINÇON, 1871

The Valpinçon family had been acquaintances of the Degas family since Edgar and Paul Valpinçon were at school together. The Valpinçons owned a large house at Menil-Hubert in Normandy, and it was on visits here that Degas first became interested in the racecourse as a subject for painting. Édouard Valpinçon also had a large art collection to which Degas was a frequent visitor. It included a nude by Jean Auguste Ingres which Degas admired above all others (a rear view of a seated bather which today is often known as the Valpinçon Bather). Degas painted this portrait of Hortense in 1871. By the painterly references to the hand movements it appears as if Hortense frequently took bites of the apple.

WOMAN WITH A VASE *(detail)*, 1872

The sitter for this portrait has not been positively identified but some people think that it shows Degas' sister-in-law, Estelle Musson. Estelle was already a widow with a young daughter when René de Gas first met her in 1865 and their marriage required a special Episcopal dispensation because they were cousins. Estelle had a tragic life; she contracted ophthalmia, which steadily caused her sight to fail, and by the time of their marriage she was incurably blind. She had five children by René but in 1878 he abandoned her, leaving New Orleans with another woman whom he eventually married. Not long after, four of the six children died. Edgar, disgusted at his brother's behaviour, refused to see René when he returned to France.

THE LIFE OF DEGAS

~1881~

Sculpture of the *Little Dancer of Fourteen Years* is exhibited.

~1882~

Paul Durand-Ruel exhibits Degas' work in London.

~1887~

Eadweard Muybridge publishes his photographic study of movement, *Animal Locomotion*.

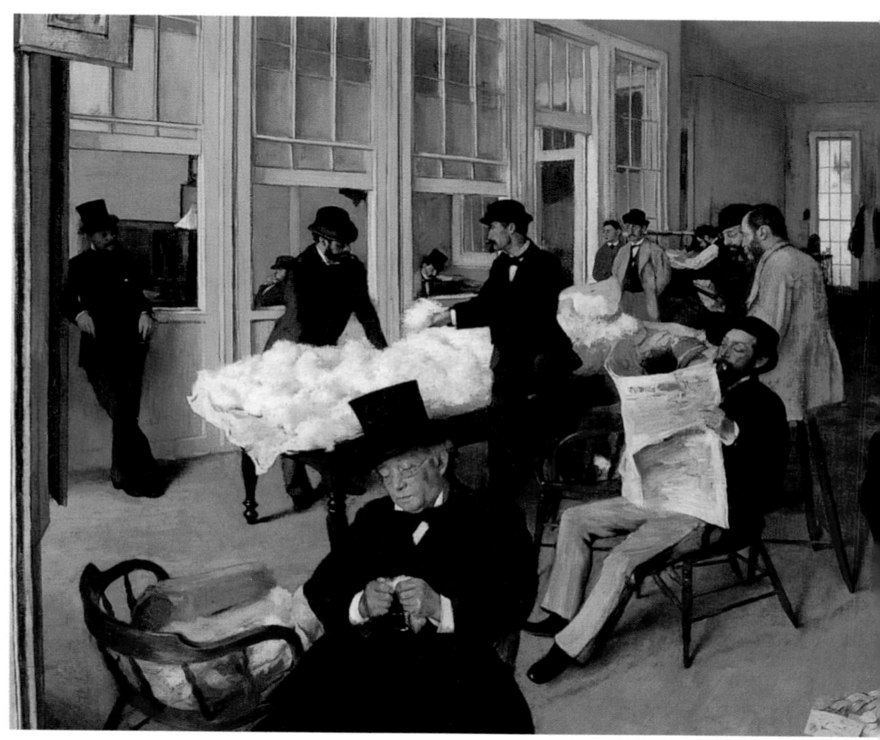

DISTANT RELATIONS

'*The ocean! How big it is! How far away from* you *I am! The* Scotia *is a British ship... I didn't know English. I still don't, and on* British *territory, even at sea, there is a coldness and a conventional distrust...'* This extract from a letter by Degas is an indication of his mood on his journey to New York aboard the Cunard Royal Mail ship, *Scotia,* in 1872. Nine years earlier Degas' brother René, had travelled to New Orleans to visit his American relatives and had fallen in love with and married his cousin Estelle. He settled in New Orleans establishing a business as a wine importer. Degas visited his relatives in 1872, staying with his uncle, Michel Musson, in a huge mansion not far from the offices of the family cotton business. Degas was clearly impressed by the town, despite the upheavals from the recent civil war. He was also impressed with the large family in which he found himself, as this extract from a letter to a friend shows. It contains a rare reference to his feelings about the possibility of marriage; *'I do not even consider that a good woman would be the enemy of this new way of life. Would a few children of my own, engendered by me, be too much? Nearly all the women here are pretty, and many include in their charms that hint of ugliness without which nothing works.'*

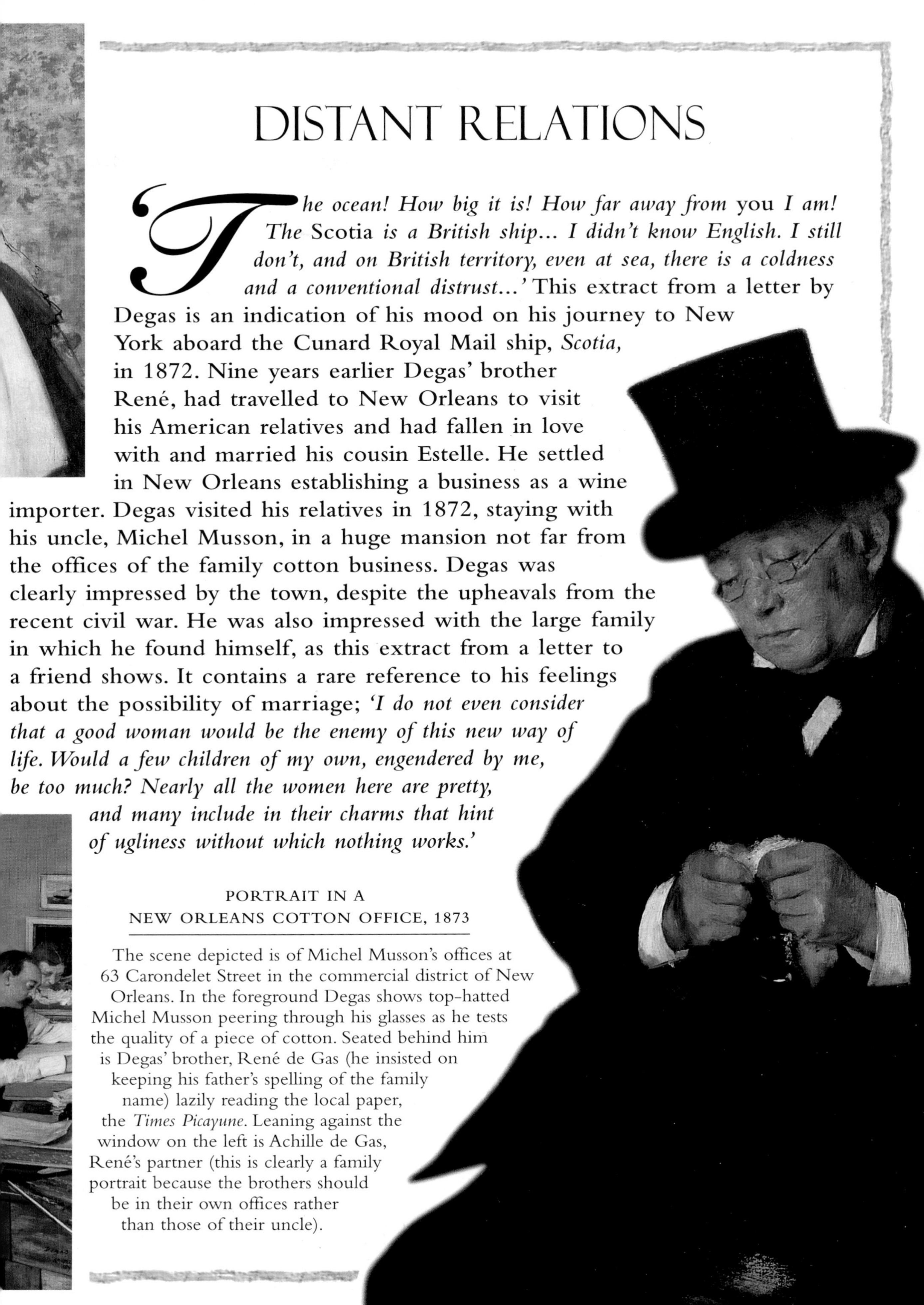

PORTRAIT IN A
NEW ORLEANS COTTON OFFICE, 1873

The scene depicted is of Michel Musson's offices at 63 Carondelet Street in the commercial district of New Orleans. In the foreground Degas shows top-hatted Michel Musson peering through his glasses as he tests the quality of a piece of cotton. Seated behind him is Degas' brother, René de Gas (he insisted on keeping his father's spelling of the family name) lazily reading the local paper, the *Times Picayune*. Leaning against the window on the left is Achille de Gas, René's partner (this is clearly a family portrait because the brothers should be in their own offices rather than those of their uncle).

THE FLÂNEUR

Degas lived and breathed Paris, and the subject of his paintings reflected the immediate world around him. When he moved out of his family home in 1865 he moved to a studio in the rue de Laval, at the southern edge of Montmartre. His subsequent moves were all around the ninth arrondissement area of Paris, enabling him to frequent the cafés and music halls around Pigalle and Montmartre. One of the most popular cafés was the Café Guerbois which became a focus for Impressionist painters. One observer recalled, *'Among the silhouettes glimpsed there every evening, in the gaslight and amid the noise of the billiard balls, I want to mention the name Degas, his very original, very Parisian face, and his humorous, bantering expression.'* Later, in the 1870s, the centre of attention moved to the Café de la Nouvelle-Athènes in Place Pigalle. Artists such as Manet and Degas, very much the Parisian flâneur, the gentleman of fashion about town, would sit for hours as the evening passed away, arguing about art.

PORTRAIT OF FRIENDS, ON THE STAGE *(detail)*, 1879

Like the café-concerts, the opera and the ballet were entertainments available to Degas in the immediate vicinity of his studio. This picture shows acquaintances Ludovic Halévy and Albert Boulanger-Cave nonchalantly chatting backstage at the opera. The right-hand figure is ruthlessly cut by the vertical line of the stage scenery in a way that suggests the viewer of this scene is just out of sight, looking around the scenery to the men deep in conversation. This compositional style which places the artist – and viewer – in the role of distant, sometimes secret, onlooker is frequently found in Degas' work.

CAFÉ-CONCERT AT THE AMBASSADEURS, 1876/7

The 'café-concert' is supposed to have started one night in 1870 when the owner of the Café d'Apollon invited indoors a group of street singers. The mixture of cheap drink and entertainment caught on and there were soon over 200 such café-concerts in Paris, ranging from dingy little bars to grand affairs such as Les Ambassadeurs, with stages and orchestras. Degas delighted in visiting the café-concerts, sketching the crowds and entertainers. A typical café-concert singer of the time was described; *'She is very female, underlining indelicate passages with a gesture and a look and pretty movements of the arms. She has a special way of holding herself, a bit like a bird.'*

The Life of Degas

~1891~
Mrs Potter Palmer pays 5,000 francs for a painting.

~1896~
Degas buys a Kodak portable camera.

~1911~
Fogg Art Museum mounts a retrospective of Degas' work.

~1912~
Louisine Havemeyer pays 478,500 francs for a painting.

~1917~
Degas dies on 27 September.

WINGS AT THE OPÉRA

Jean Béraud

French dance in the 1870s was a decadent affair. The great Russian choreographers were yet to arrive, and the ballets performed at the Opéra were for the most part minor entertainments. 'Gentlemen' were permitted backstage where they could flirt with the dancers, and make assignations for after the performance. The wealthier followers sometimes insisted on roles for their mistresses, regardless of talent. The famous composer Hector Berlioz referred to it as 'a house of assignation'. One critic summed it up: *'The man of fashion at the Opéra, with his box or his stall, his favourite dancer, his opéra glasses, and his right of entry backstage, has a horror of anything… artistic, which must be listened to, respected, or requires an effort to be understood.'*

THE ABSINTHE DRINKER, 1876

This painting, originally entitled *Dans un Café* (In a Café), caused an uproar when it was exhibited in Brighton in 1876. The subject matter was controversial because absinthe was deemed responsible at the time for the high rate of alcoholism among the working classes of Paris. No matter that this was an image of real life; the gallery-going public considered it shocking and did not want to be confronted with it. The two sad and downcast figures depicted were in fact friends of Degas.

FAMOUS IMAGES

Two of Degas' best-known paintings are *The Absinthe Drinker* and *Miss La La at the Circus Fernando.* Both reflect his determination to represent the world around him as realistically as possible. Degas said he wanted to portray people in their customary, typical attitudes, with facial expressions matching bodily postures. He recorded fleeting moments, capturing the everyday instances of modern life both in its grim detail and in its gaudy colours. His drawings and paintings combine acute observation with masterful draughtsmanship in the tradition of Ingres. Nothing around him escaped his critical gaze: the café-concert singer, the circus performer, the laundry woman, the ballet dancer. Degas would capture these scenes of modern Paris life in sketchbooks and work up finished pictures in oil or pastel in his studio. Degas' work is famous for the unusual angles he presents onto his scenes. *Miss La La* is a good example but many of his pictures present the spectator with a view of a person or subject which is unconventional – we are more familiar with such angles today as a result of a casual photographic image rather than a planned canvas. This sense of immediacy in his work was planned. Degas' good friend and critic Edmond Duranty described it as *'the sense of modernity as it is caught on the wing'*.

The painter Marcellin Desboutin posed as the male down-and-out, dressed in his usual battered hat and with his clay pipe, despite the fact that he was never known to be anything other than sober.

His female companion, apparently lost in thought and with the glass of green absinthe in front of her, is actress and fashion model Ellen Andrée, considered something of a beauty and the subject of many portraits by artists such as Manet, Renoir and Gervex. Andrée complained that Degas had 'massacred' her in the painting and was also unhappy that he placed the glass in front of her rather than Desboutin.

THE BLACK VENUS

Miss La La was known as the 'Black Venus' (she was part African). Her act involved feats of strength with her teeth and jaws. It was at the climax of one of these acts, when Miss La La was being hauled up high into the dome of the amphitheatre at the end of a rope held in her teeth, that Degas chose to paint her.

MISS LA LA AT THE CIRCUS FERNANDO, 1879

Degas decided on the most challenging depiction possible, composing his picture around a view of Miss La La from below as she rises up into the rib-vaulted cupola of the circus. Degas made countless sketches in preparation for the painting, and struggled to achieve the correct perspective for the figure as she is hauled up, rotating as she rises. Degas tried many different poses before settling on the one that conveys the soaring, almost flying figure, her face upturned and her arms and legs striking a ballet position as she begins the dangerous and exciting stunt.

A PROBLEM OF PERSPECTIVE

The view from below looking upwards (known by the Italian renaissance artists as 'sotto in su') was a compositional technique used to create a sense of dramatic movement and space. Degas later confessed that in order to paint the background architecture he called on help from a professional perspecteur who often assisted painters struggling with mathematical perspective.

CIRCUS FERNANDO

The Circus Fernando opened in 1875 in an amphitheatre in the Boulevard Rochechouart, near Place Pigalle, and a short walk from Degas' studio. It attracted artists local to the area, such as Degas and Renoir, who were often found sketching in the circus. However, only one major work by Degas resulted from his visits. Circus Fernando was renamed Circus Medrano from 1890 onwards.

WHAT DO DEGAS' PAINTINGS SAY?

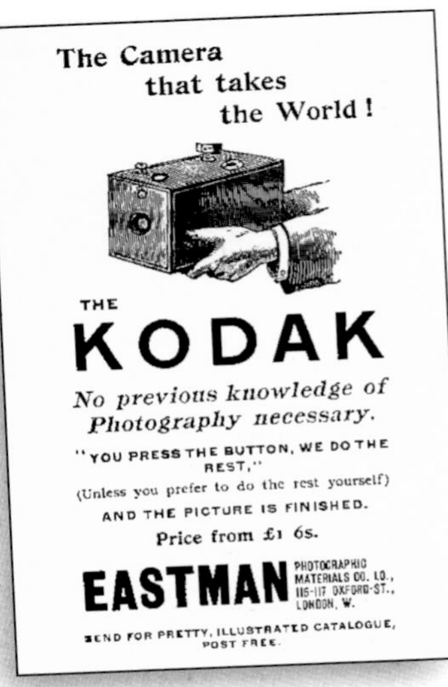

A NEW PASSION

In 1888, the American George Eastman formed the Kodak company which marketed cheap cameras using flexible roll film. Degas bought a portable Kodak camera in 1896 which he took great pride in carrying with him. About that time a friend wrote: *'Degas is abandoning everything in favour of his new lust for photography.'*

Observation was everything to an artist and Degas' obsession with it bordered on the voyeuristic. By the 1870s, a new way of observing was available; the camera. Degas became an enthusiastic photographer and had no worries about using this new technology to help him with his art. In fact it changed the way he looked at one of his favourite subjects, the racehorse. Degas made many sketches of jockeys and horses at the track, but he also relied heavily on existing sources such as English sporting prints. Another source to which Degas turned was the artist Jean-Louis Meissonier. His paintings, which included horses in their subject matter, were famous for their 'correctness'. In 1878 the journal *La Nature* published Eadweard Muybridge's experiments of freeze-frame photographs of moving horses. They showed clearly that artists were incorrect when they depicted horses with all four legs outstretched and not touching the ground. Degas was aware of Muybridge's work and may even have attended a presentation he gave in Paris.

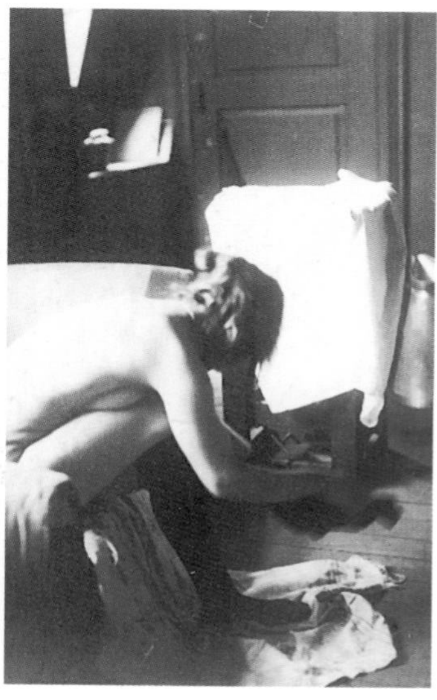

SEATED NUDE c.1896

Photograph attributed to Degas.

A STEEPLECHASE

John Herring

John Herring was an English artist whose painting *Steeple Chase Cracks* was owned by Degas' father. It can be seen on the wall in the background of Degas' painting entitled *Sulking* (1869).

LE DEFILE, 1879

'And for the manipulations of a bet
He must begin - a dark horse on the field
Nervously naked in its silken robe.'

These lines from Degas' notebook show that he attempted to capture the skittish elegance of the racehorse in sonnet form as well as in oil on canvas. As far as Degas was concerned the subject was not just about capturing equine grace and beauty; he enjoyed the social occasion of the races. Although many of his sketches show that he worked directly from his subject, it is quite clear that the highly finished drawings and paintings were made in his studio. There he had a dummy horse so that the jockeys who posed for him could adopt the correct posture.

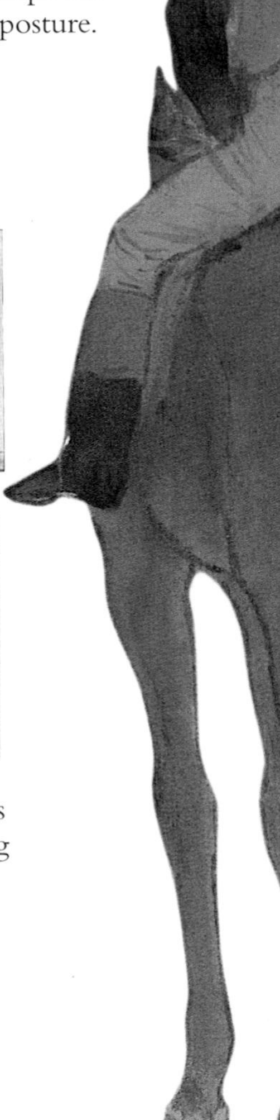

PHOTO SEQUENCE OF RACEHORSE *c.*1884-5

Eadweard Muybridge

Eadweard Muybridge carried out a number of experiments from the 1870s onwards which involved taking a rapid series of still photographs of moving animals (and humans) to show the successive stages of locomotion. The animals were photographed against a plain background in order to see clearly the various stages of movement. His work was known in Paris in the 1870s but he became famous after the publication of *Animal Locomotion* in 1887, which became a standard textbook on animal and human movement. The book was widely used by artists to assist in the composition of their paintings.

WHAT DO DEGAS' PAINTINGS SAY?

In later life Degas made countless drawings and paintings of women as they bathed and groomed themselves. Critics express different views about these works in which his models are invariably naked. Some are of the opinion that the male scrutiny to which the women are subject means they are exploited as objects. Others argue that Degas is one of the few artists who does not reduce the female form to a sexual spectacle, but depicts his subjects as believable people going about their everyday tasks. They are shown in awkward positions as they climb from baths or brush their hair. Some of his most intimate pictures are of women combing their hair: an activity that can be read as both banal and tedious, as well as sensuous. In Degas' times it was normal for women to keep their hair long but pinned and coiled out of sight. For 19th-century women the task of washing, brushing and combing long hair was a laborious one, often accomplished with the help of a mother, sister or servant. For men of the time just the thought of such activity, of seeing women with their hair loose, was enough to create excitement.

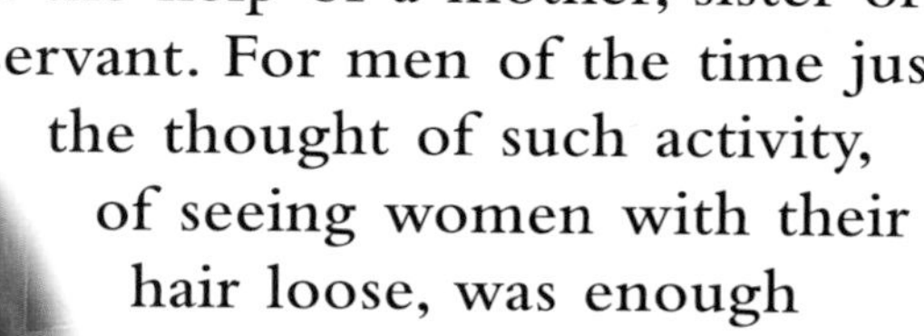

WOMAN COMBING HER HAIR

Kitagawa Utamaro

The depiction of the act of combing hair has a long tradition in art. Examples can be seen in European painting of the Renaissance period (Titian) and later, such as the picture below by Ingres. It also occurs in art of the Far East, such as the colour wood-block print above by Kitagawa Utamaro, made in 1803 and set in the floating world of the pleasure-houses of Edo.

THE TURKISH BATH

Jean Auguste Dominique Ingres

WOMAN COMBING HER HAIR, 1885/6

The novelist Émile Zola, an acquaintance of Degas, admitted to being excited merely by the sound of hairpins falling from loosened tresses into a metal washbasin. One of Degas' models is reported to have remarked of Degas to a friend, *'He is odd Monsieur – he spent the four hours of my posing session combing my hair.'* There are also signs of his interest in long hair in one of his very first paintings, *The Suffering of the City of New Orleans*, painted in 1865. Although Degas never expressed sentiments similar to those of Zola, he did admit to a fascination for observing and faithfully recording the human form and all of its activities. In conversation with the Irish writer George Moore, in 1891, Degas said: *'It's the human animal taking care of its body, a female cat licking herself. Hitherto the nude has always been represented in poses which presuppose an audience, but these women of mine are honest, simple folk, unconcerned by any other interests than those involved in their physical condition.'*

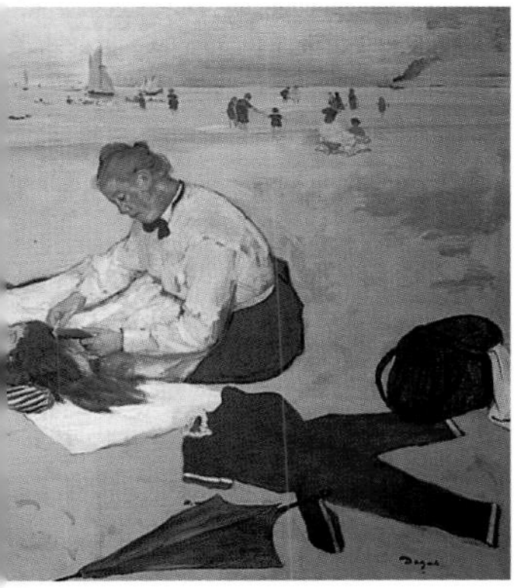

AT THE BEACH, 1876

In this painting Degas portrays a young girl lying on the beach. It would appear from the costume laid out nearby, and from the figures in the sea in the distance, that she has just returned from a swim. A woman (the dress suggests her nurse) bends over the girl, and carefully combs her hair. The young girl toys idly with the edge of the parasol, patiently allowing the woman to attend to her. The painting was executed in 1876, and at first glance would seem to be very much in the Impressionist style. Degas was exhibiting with the Impressionists at that time, and the subject matter – outdoors, the beach, the feeling of immediacy – fitted well. But Degas let it be known that the models *'sat on my flannel vest spread out on the studio floor'* and the background is clearly taken from an earlier pastel entitled *On the Channel Coast.* The hair-combing scene at the centre of the painting was a theme that Degas would return to again over the next 20 years, increasingly depicting it as a very private scene behind closed doors. Degas may have intended a small detail to be deliberately amusing; the smoke from the two steamships on the horizon blows in opposite directions.

SPONTANEITY

In the foreground a dancer who appears to be perched on a piano reaches awkwardly to scratch her back; her right shoulder half obscures the face of another who fiddles with her earring. These details help to capture the impression of spontaneity.

THE INVISIBLE OBSERVER

Although Degas' work covered a wide range of subjects, he is probably best known for his images of dancers. It is estimated that Degas made approximately 1,500 paintings, pastels, prints and drawings of dancers. Very few of the pictures, however, depict the performance itself. Most of the views are not from the auditorium looking onto the stage but from behind the scenes, and particularly of the ballet rehearsal. There was no great tradition of the ballet as a subject for painting although many respectable artists had made portraits of famous dancers in costume. The ballet was however a very popular subject for the 19th-century mass-market, with many cheap lithographs depicting pretty dancers with tiny feet and coy gazes. Degas would certainly have been aware of the popularity of these prints and the prospect of potential sales may have encouraged him to consider the ballet as a subject. Entertainments at the Opera House would have been an obvious attraction given its proximity to Degas' studio. He was drawn to making observations backstage at the *Foyer de la Danse*, where men mixed with the dancers, as well as the stage where the dancers performed.

In the immediate foreground Degas has included a small dog and a watering can. Both serve to enhance perspective, reinforced by the lines of the floorboards which narrow towards the back of the picture.

THE DANCE CLASS, 1874

One of Degas' earlier paintings of the ballet is *The Dance Class*. It contains all the elements that fascinated Degas and to which he returned time and time again. The painting captures the rehearsal room atmosphere, full of movement and activity, chattering dancers adjusting their costumes and yawning and scratching, while the teacher watches a dancer go through her steps.

In the far corner, to which the viewer's eye is drawn by the sharply angled perspective, dancers wait with their mothers who fuss over their daughter's costumes. The way the scene is painted reinforces Degas' role as invisible observer. The dancers literally have their backs to the artist as if unaware of his presence.

INFLUENCED BY PHOTOGRAPHY

The apparently arbitrary framing of the scene, which cuts in half the dancer who stands on the far right of the picture, and the manner in which figures overlap each other, is typical of Degas' work. The painting appears to mimic the 'snapshot' effect of a photograph.

The dancer with her back to the viewer, and the empty space at the bottom right of the picture, serve to accentuate the sense of deep space in the painting. This effect is often created by the lens of a camera but seldom experienced by the human eye. Degas' interest in photography would have helped him achieve the very carefully composed image.

The male figure at the centre of *The Dance Class* is Jules Perrot, choreographer and ballet master. He had been a famous dancer in the 1830s and had moved to the Bolshoi Theatre in St Petersburg in 1840 where he stayed until 1849.

THE DANCER IN FOCUS

The American art collector Louisine Havemeyer asked Degas why he chose to paint the ballet, to which Degas is reported to have replied, *'Because it is all that is left us of the combined movement of the Greeks.'* The continuing belief in the classical tradition is again in evidence. Like the Greeks, Degas was concerned with the human figure; its strength, poise and balance. He made literally hundreds of drawings showing the figure in every posture. His fascination with the dancer was an excuse to observe the female form in action and at rest, in tension as it stretched to exercise, and in relaxation or boredom waiting for the next movement in rehearsals.

DANCER READING PAPER, 1878/9

This delightful sketch shows one of the dancers standing by the stove reading the newspaper, waiting perhaps for the dance teacher to call her for the next rehearsal, or for Monsieur Degas to call her for another pose. Even at rest she is standing only as a dancer could, her left foot out-turned, back straight and perfectly poised. There is an intimacy in this glimpse, caught in a moment of distraction, that underlines Degas' understanding of the world of the dancer. Most of the girls came from working-class families, often as young as seven. They were pushed by ambitious mothers despite the Paris ballet's seedy reputation. However, if the dancers were successful they could move on from being *rats* (students) to members of the corps de ballet, then *petits sujets* (soloists) to the fame of *première danseuse* (principal dancers).

DANCER OF THE CORPS DE BALLET *c.*1895

This photograph, owned by Degas, was one of many either taken by the artist or arranged by him. It is known that he worked from his photographs but what is unclear is why the originals are collodion glass plates, a photographic process which by the 1890s had long been replaced by newer developments, such as the flexible photographic film and different processing methods. They are however very beautiful images reminiscent of Degas' own renderings of dancers with areas of soft tones leading into sharp contrast and focused detail.

L'ÉTOILE, 1876

In this picture of the 'star', or *première danseuse,* Degas chooses a view from the auditorium towards the stage rather than the more common backstage view. He rarely depicted performances, preferring to attend the rehearsals or have models dressed in costume in his studio. Degas uses a technique known as *repoussoir* (from the French verb *repousser,* to push back) which can often be seen in his paintings. This technique involves a strongly defined (or in focus) person in the foreground, often off-centre, which deflects the viewer's attention towards the rear and enhances the illusion of depth. In this painting the viewer's eye is drawn towards the anonymous male figure watching from the wings. It is also possible to see a reference here to Degas' own position as hidden viewer.

BALLET SHOE FOUND IN DEGAS' STUDIO

Artist Georges Jeanniot described how Degas showed him a dancer's foot. *'He discussed the special shape of the satin shoes held on by silk cords which lace up the ankles... Suddenly he snatched up a piece of charcoal and in the margin of my sheet drew the structure of the model's foot with a few long black lines; then with his finger he added a few shadows and half-tones; the foot was alive, perfectly modelled, its form released from banality by its deliberate and yet spontaneous treatment.'*

BOX OF PASTELS FOUND IN DEGAS' STUDIO

Degas bought his pastels from artist suppliers such as S. Macle, who provided this box which was found in his studio. Pastels are made from mixing coloured pigments with a binder such as gum and pressing the mixture into moulds. Degas is said to have soaked his pastel sticks in water then allowed them to dry in the sun, thereby testing the permanence of the pigment. His suspicions were caused by the rapid development of new colours which were coming onto the market at that time, many of which proved to be less than satisfactory.

LEAVING THE BATH, 1895

Despite Degas' admiration of traditional conventions and the classical style, he was an enthusiast of pastels, a medium considered decorative and frivolous by most artists, suitable only for *'the brilliant tints of a young girl, the flesh of a child'*. Many of his pastel works appear to defy his own rules about the importance of line and drawing as the dusty colours explore the shape, tone and hue of the subject. However, the medium is ideal for a draughtsman such as Degas because a stick of pastel is both for drawing lines and colouring areas. Typically a work began as a drawing and then transformed through veils of local colour, often worked into the paper with fingers. Sometimes the image defies any attempt to identify preliminary sketches or lines, and appears to comprise a single veil of different colours rubbed and merged together. Degas often worked on tracing paper, an unusual choice because the hard shiny surface is particularly unreceptive to pastel. After drawing, hatching and colouring, the image was often fixed with a dilute varnish, sprayed onto the surface, which prevented the soft colours from smudging. Degas then returned to work on top of the fixed surface with more layers of colour which were in turn fixed. Occasionally Degas would use unusual and extreme interventions such as steam, or would scrape away the surface of the paper to get the desired effect.

HOW WERE THE PAINTINGS MADE?

Degas is acknowledged as one of the greatest draughtsmen of the 19th century. He was a great innovator, experimenting with new techniques to produce the effects on canvas and paper that he was looking for. His ability to represent his subject with extraordinary accuracy, an ability made possible by years of study, gave him the freedom to use a huge range of materials with tremendous confidence. These materials included orthodox media such as oil on canvas, pastel on paper, drawings and watercolours. They also included processes that he devised himself, for example the monotype (single prints), distemper on linen (powdered colours mixed with size) and painting with essence (oil paint thinned with turpentine). Some works, such as *Rehearsal of the Ballet on the Stage*, he painted in watercolour, gouache, oils and finished with pen and ink.

Standing Dancer, from Behind
(essence on pink paper)

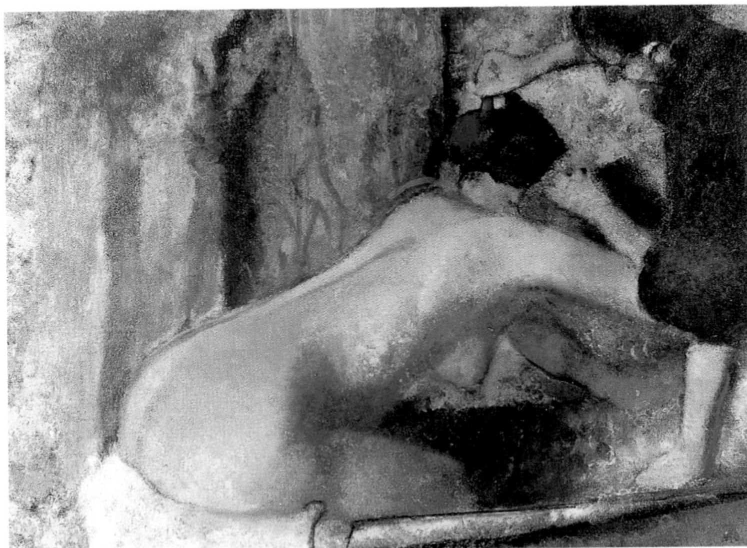

WOMAN AT HER BATH, 1892

Degas' later pastel and oil paintings took on a vibrancy of colour which one observer described as *'the marriage and adultery of colours'*. The intensity of colour reached new heights as his techniques enabled him to create layer upon layer just as the great masters had achieved colour luminosity in oils by building up successive layers of transparent colour. His oil paintings even looked like pastels, with dry paint surfaces and areas of colour that resembled chalk. Critics commenting on his pictures described *'a blue not seen by vulgar eyes'* and *'colours burnt by light, disappearing in passages of greenish flame, falling into embers and pink ashes'*.

HOW WERE THE PAINTINGS MADE?

Degas was aware of the oil painting processes used by artists of preceding generations. His respect for such traditions gave rise to problems whereas he felt free and unencumbered by historical tradition when using pastel. Degas eventually found his own way of working in oils that enabled his own inventiveness to build upon traditional methods of painting. He advised the painter Rouart to make a traditional groundwork, let it dry in the open air for a few months, then glaze with colours in the manner of masters such as Titian. But Degas himself used brightly coloured grounds which shone through the subsequent layers of paint, instead of underpainting the canvas in a groundwork of the standard brownish colour (intended to provide the underlying tones). In complete contradiction to his advice to Rouart he also bought lengths of coarse canvas and washed colour direct onto the unprimed surface, then brushed thick paint across it so the dry paint caught on the coarse weave. Painting in oils, the 'cursed medium' as Degas called it, was always a challenge for the master draughtsman.

Palette used by Degas.

STANDING WOMAN IN A BATH TUB, *c.*1895

The monotype has been in use for hundreds of years but is more or less ignored by artists. Degas 'discovered' the technique in 1874, and in the following years produced hundreds of prints. The monotype is simply a print created by painting an image in oils or inks onto a smooth plate (Degas used copper or zinc) which is then pressed against an absorbent paper, resulting in the transfer of the image onto the paper. It is called monotype because only one (mono) image can be printed. In some cases the whole plate would be covered with a layer of thick ink and by wiping away parts of the ink with a rag, Degas would reveal a 'negative' image. When the plate was printed onto paper the areas of ink remaining on the plate would produce the 'positive' (dark) tones of the print as in this example (right).

AFTER THE BATH, WOMAN DRYING HERSELF, *c.*1896

This work was considered by Degas to be unfinished. It appears to be painted in the brownish-reds of the *ébauche* (underpainting) and possibly set aside to dry, but never taken up again by Degas. The posture of the model is far from expectations of normal everyday bathing and drying. Instead we are presented with a torso which stretches the back into a contorted pose. Degas' interest is clearly both to observe the form and musculature of the back, through photography, and to capture the same in oils.

AFTER THE BATH

This is one of Degas' most striking photographs and quite clearly links to his painting made at the same time. He complained that he could get nothing except black paper from the development of his photographs taken in the evening and reluctantly used some of his precious daytime hours, normally reserved for painting, in order to get sufficient light to register a photographic image. He sometimes used carefully placed gas lamps to 'paint' his subject in light before making the long photographic exposure. This photograph, like many, has carefully controlled light which falls from above (probably from the tall studio windows) across the back of his model, throwing into relief the curvature of the spine and shoulder blades.

THE AUDIENCE & THE CRITICS

Degas' reputation grew in the 1870s as he emerged as one of the main exhibitors with the Impressionist group. He did not have financial worries like some of his fellow artists but his income from his banking family was not large, as some supposed. Degas preferred to keep his pictures unless circumstances necessitated a sale, and then he sold his work directly to the many visitors to his studio or through established art dealers. He shunned the system of one-man exhibitions which had worked so well for his contemporary, Claude Monet, and he refused to exhibit at the official Salon. This distaste for promotion and commercialism was partly as a result of the mauling he suffered at the hands of the critics, and partly to do with his privileged upbringing. One consequence was that few works by Degas were in circulation, and collectors actively sought his paintings. Towards the end of his life his pictures were selling for hundreds of thousands of francs.

PHOTOGRAPH OF THEO VAN GOGH

Theo van Gogh was a dealer for the Boussod et Valadon gallery. He was one of many visitors to Degas' studio in the rue Victor Masse who wished to promote the artist's work. In 1888 Theo van Gogh persuaded Degas to exhibit a series of pastel studies of bathers. The pictures caused a good deal of excitement and a handful of the pictures were sold. Theo was a great promoter of the Impressionist's work, spurred on by the support he gave to his brother, Vincent.

DURAND-RUEL EXHIBITION AT THE GRAFTON GALLERIES, LONDON IN 1905

Paul Durand-Ruel (left) was the driving force behind the Durand-Ruel galleries. He arranged for the Impressionist works, including those of Degas, to be exhibited in Paris, London and New York, and it was this final venue in America that established the group as a commercial success. More and more rich American collectors were drawn to this new style of painting and began to visit the Paris studios in their eagerness to buy. Success did take time for Durand-Ruel, but in the 1890s he had established a gallery in New York and works by artists such as Degas were changing hands quickly.

THE TUB, 1886

Critics did not on the whole approve of Degas' pastels of bathers when they first appeared in 1886. One reviewer wrote: *'The woman crouching in a tub, pressing a sponge to her back… these drawings are not done to inspire a passion for women, nor a desire for the flesh… Monsieur Degas, studying them at close range, decomposing their movements, has given them the alarming character of tormented creatures, straining anatomies distorted by the violent exercises they are compelled to perform.'* The English, who were more accustomed to the chocolate box imagery of Victorian women, were direct in their views. London reviews of Degas' dance pictures referred to *'danseuses scantily endowed with beauty… arch, sly, vain and ugly ballet girls.'*

PORTRAIT OF MRS HAVEMEYER

Mary Cassatt

One of the most influential collectors of Impressionist works was Louisine Havemeyer, wife of Henry Osborne Havemeyer, head of the American Sugar-Refining Company. Both Henry and Louisine were avid art collectors but Louisine continued after her husband's death in 1907. In 1912 she paid 478,500 francs for Degas' *Dancers Practising at the Bar.* This portrait is by the female Impressionist painter Mary Cassatt who was a childhood friend of Louisine Havemeyer. When she died in 1929, Louisine bequeathed 36 works by Degas to the Metropolitan Museum of Art in New York.

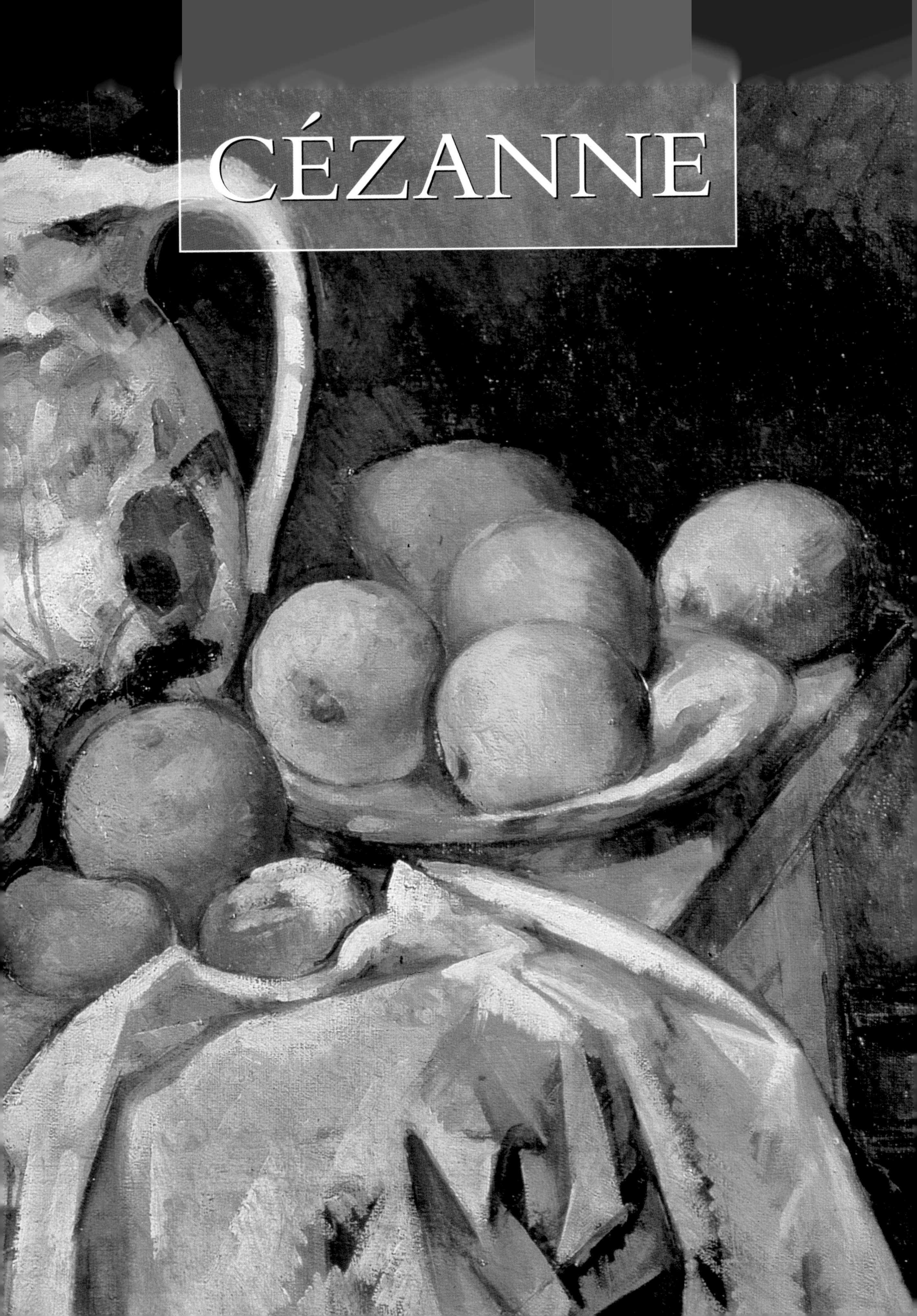
CÉZANNE

THE WORLD OF CÉZANNE

Paul Cézanne was born on the 19 January 1839 in Aix-en-Provence in the south of France. Paul was the eldest of three children born to Louis-Auguste Cézanne and Anne-Élisabeth Aubert. Paul's father made enough money as a felt-hat trader to become a banker, founding the Cézanne and Cabassol Bank in Aix in 1848. Paul grew up in a secure well-to-do family home with his two sisters enjoying the pleasant climate and attractive countryside surrounding Aix. When he was 13 years old he attended the Collège Bourbon in Aix as a boarder, and it was here he met Émile Zola who was to become a lifelong friend. Cézanne and Zola, together with a third friend Jean Baptiste Baille, became known to their school friends as the 'Inseparables' who enjoyed nothing more than long walks in the countryside, fishing and swimming in the nearby river Arc. Cézanne, encouraged by his father to study Law, eventually enrolled at the university of Aix.

AIX-EN-PROVENCE, *c.*1900

Approximately 32 kilometres (20 miles) north of the Mediterranean port of Marseilles and 650 kilometres (400 miles) south of Paris, Aix-en-Provence was a provincial town which proved idyllic for the growing child but a conservative backwater for the young intellectual. Émile Zola left for Paris as soon as he had finished at the Collège Bourbon in 1858, while Cézanne stayed on to enrol at the university and attend life-drawing classes at the local free drawing school. Cézanne's father had decided that legal training was the best course for his son and of most help to the prosperous Cézanne Bank. It was obvious to the young Cézanne, however, that a career as a lawyer was not what he wanted, and he dreamt of joining his friend Zola in Paris and becoming an artist.

PAUL CÉZANNE

It was quite clear that Cézanne was not going to settle down at university in Aix to study Law, nor was he going to follow his father's footsteps into the family bank. Encouraged by Émile Zola, Cézanne decided to head for Paris and try his hand as an artist. Eventually Cézanne's father gave him his blessing and Cézanne travelled to Paris in 1861 to spend the summer with Zola. This was an unhappy time. Cézanne felt an outsider and did not feel comfortable with the sophisticated ways of the city dwellers. He missed the countryside of Provence and after his application to join the École des Beaux-Arts in Paris was turned down he returned, dejected, to Aix. It would not be long however before the urge returned and he made plans to return to Paris with the financial support of his father.

ONE OF FOUR MURALS FROM THE SALON OF THE JAS DE BOUFFAN, 1859

The Jas de Bouffan was generally in a poor state of repair when the Cézanne family moved there, and Paul was given permission to paint on the walls of one of the rooms. In 1859 Cézanne painted a series of murals of the four seasons. These paintings are the earliest known works of Cézanne. The elongated female figures depicted in the murals show Cézanne's knowledge of art of previous generations. They show the distinct influence of artists such as the 16th-century Italian Sandro Botticelli, and Cézanne himself recognizes his debt by signing the paintings, not in his own name, but that of Ingres, who was famed for his academic style.

HOUSE AND FARM AT THE JAS DE BOUFFAN *(detail)*, 1885/7

In 1859 Louis-Auguste Cézanne purchased a fine 18th-century house with surrounding grounds situated close to the centre of Aix. The house had formerly belonged to the Governor of Provence and was called the *Jas de Bouffan* (House of the Wind).

INFLUENCES & EARLY WORKS

In 1862 Cézanne settled in Paris. Like all aspiring artists he was a frequent visitor to the Louvre where he spent hours sitting in front of paintings meticulously copying the great masters. This was the established way of learning how to paint and Cézanne was no exception. Gradually he discovered the works of living artists such as Eugène Delacroix who was a great source of inspiration for artists of Cézanne's generation. Delacroix symbolized rebellion against the Classical art which dominated the art schools at the time, led by the great French artist and master draughtsman Jean Auguste Dominique Ingres. The Romantic artists, led by Delacroix, considered colour to be more important than draughtsmanship and favoured exotic subject matter over the traditional subjects depicted by the followers of Ingres. The École des Beaux-Arts taught in the Classical tradition still favoured by the critics and by the public, but it was increasingly out of touch with the new generation of artists. The up-and-coming painters no longer sought the advice and approval of the established system of teaching and they were becoming dissatisfied with the official annual exhibition of paintings at the Salon.

THE STRANGLED WOMAN (*detail*), *c.*1870/2

In his early works painted during the 1860s Cézanne's rapid fusion of brushstrokes and colour borrow from the work of Delacroix, but also appear similar to the pictures of Honoré Daumier, an artist whose cartoons were full of biting political satire. The dark earthy realism of his solid figures could equally owe a debt to Gustave Courbet whose work would have been known to the young Cézanne. Cézanne experimented with different painterly styles during this period just as he chose to depict a wide range of subject matter, from imaginary scenes of violence to still life.

APOTHEOSIS OF DELACROIX, *c.*1870/2

Cézanne made his palette of colours deliberately bright in emulation of Delacroix. Of colour he said; '*Pure drawing is an abstraction. Line and modelling do not count; drawing and outline are not distinct, since everything in nature has colour... by the very fact of painting one draws. The accuracy of tone gives simultaneously the light and shape of the object, and the more harmonious the colour, the more the drawing becomes precise.*'

THE DEATH OF SARDANAPALUS *Eugène Delacroix*

When Delacroix painted this picture in 1829 he was angrily attacked by the art establishment for his use of brilliant colour, exotic and dramatic subject matter, and free handling of the paint, which was seen to be 'anti-French' in its rejection of French Classicism. In 1832 he visited north Africa and this opened up a whole new field of subject matter as well as heightening his appreciation of colour. He also used literary sources of inspiration including Byron, Scott and Shakespeare, and his way of painting broke new ground enabling the Realist artists to follow.

Cézanne made a number of copies of Delacroix's paintings as well as making his own pictures which also contained images of violence such as *The Abduction, The Murder, The Strangled Woman* and *The Autopsy*.

THE HOUSE OF
DR GACHET AT AUVERS, *c.*1873

Cézanne was encouraged by Pissarro to move to a small village near Pontoise called Auvers-sur-Oise. Cézanne stayed with the eccentric art enthusiast Dr. Gachet who was a great supporter of the young artists. Pissarro and Cézanne painted landscapes in the pretty countryside.

INFLUENCES & EARLY WORKS

In Paris, Cézanne mixed with the most modern, adventurous painters and intellectuals who discussed their ideas about art and literature in the Paris cafés, particularly the Café Guerbois in the Batignolles district of Paris. The painter Camille Pissarro became a good friend and introduced Cézanne to artists such as Manet, Monet and Renoir. Cézanne however did not feel at ease in this company, and complained in a letter *'I am just wasting my time in every respect... just don't go imagining that I shall become a Parisian...'* In 1863 the 'Salon des Refusés' was set up to give the public the opportunity to see the works of artists rejected from the official Salon. The picture that caused the greatest sensation at the Salon des Refusés was *Le Déjeuner sur l'Herbe* by Édouard Manet. The works of Manet and Courbet attempted to be true to life, depicting ordinary scenes of everyday life, *'bringing art into contact with the common people.'* Cézanne submitted a number of paintings to the Salon, all of which were rejected.

THE CUTTING, 1870

Cézanne travelled between Paris and his family home in Aix. In 1869 he met his future wife, Hortense Fiquet, who modelled for him when he was working in Paris, and they began living together. In 1870 they moved to the fishing village of L'Estaque, near Marseilles, to avoid the Franco-Prussian war. Cézanne became obsessed with painting the rocky Mediterranean landscape. Around this time he painted the landscape of a railway cutting near Aix. In the distance, behind the cutting, towers the Mont Sainte-Victoire, this feature of the Aix countryside was to dominate Cézanne's painting for the rest of his life.

THE HOUSE OF THE HANGED MAN

This painting was made in 1873 when Cézanne was heavily influenced by the Impressionist style. The painting reveals Cézanne's continuing obsession with representing solidity of form. Heavy brushstrokes give it a physicality anchoring the imagery in the landscape, rather than relying on colour to depict light, as in the works of the Impressionist painters. *The House of the Hanged Man* was exhibited at the first Impressionist exhibition where it was purchased by Count Armand Doria for the sum of 300 francs.

PHOTO OF PISSARRO & CÉZANNE

Camille Pissarro (left) had been friends with Cézanne since they first met in Paris at the Académie Suisse in 1861. Pissarro, who was 10 years older than Cézanne, persuaded him to try painting outdoors. This *en plein air* way of painting was favoured by Pissarro and became the hallmark of the Impressionist painters. They believed it was essential to get close to their subjects, to capture what they saw with immediacy. They concerned themselves with the fleeting effects of light on the subject, and rejected the studio-bound method of painting. Pissarro had a profound influence on Cézanne's painting in the early 1870s and was equally influential on other painters of the day. Pissarro was the only artist to exhibit in all eight Impressionist exhibitions.

THE LIFE OF CÉZANNE

~1839~

Paul Cézanne born on the 19 January in Aix-en-Provence, eldest of three children.

~1844~

Paul's parents, Louis-Auguste Cézanne and Anne-Élisabeth Aubert are married.

~1852~

Attends the Collège Bourbon where he meets Émile Zola and Jean Baptiste Baille. The three become best friends.

~1857~

Attends the drawing school in Aix.

~1859~

Attends the University of Aix to study law.

~1861~

Spends the summer in Paris studying art at the Académie Suisse where he meets Pissarro.

Reluctantly returns to Aix to work in the family bank.

~1862~

Cézanne gives up work and his legal studies to return to Paris with a modest allowance from his father.

~1863~

Attends the Académie Suisse once more and meets Impressionist painters Sisley, Monet and Renoir.

~1866~

Submits work to the Paris Salon but is rejected.

THE FLOOR STRIPPERS *Gustave Caillebotte*

La Deuxième Exposition (The Second Exhibition) of Impressionism was held at the art dealer Durand-Ruel's gallery at 11 rue le Peletier in Paris from 11 April to 9 May 1876. One of the paintings that caused the greatest sensation was *The Floor Strippers* by Gustave Caillebotte. Caillebotte was an extremely talented and wealthy artist. He extended his interest in painting not only by buying artwork, but by exhibiting it alongside his own. This painting depicts workmen stripping the floor of his new Paris apartment.

FOUR GIRLS ON A BRIDGE

Edvard Munch

Artists from all over the world flocked to Paris in the 1870s and 1880s as its reputation as a vibrant exciting city with the most modern trends in art spread. Wealthy Americans travelled to Paris, some to collect this new art, some to become artists themselves. A young Norwegian painter named Edvard Munch travelled to Paris and much of his formative youth was spent in the city. By 1892 Munch had attracted enough interest to be able to hold a large Exhibition of his work in Berlin. His art was very influential and he soon became a powerful factor in the growth of the Expressionist movement. Munch had himself been influenced in Paris by the deeply personal vision expressed in the works of Gauguin and van Gogh.

THE ART OF CÉZANNE'S DAY

Early in his career Cézanne exhibited alongside artists such as Manet, Whistler and Pissarro. In 1877 Cézanne showed 16 paintings at the third Impressionist exhibition which was received with a torrent of criticism. Unlike many of his contemporaries Cézanne spent a great deal of time away from Paris, often in his home town of Aix and the nearby Mediterranean village of L'Estaque. Meanwhile fellow Paris-based artists such as Monet, Degas and Manet continued to defy the critics with their determination to pursue the new style of painting and sweep away the traditional values of art. Manet's paintings of naked women depicted in recognizable settings shocked a public who were used to art which placed them in the socially acceptable realm of classical mythology. Degas' abrupt framing of everyday scenes copied the photographic 'snapshot' which was challenging art as a visual record. Monet's *Impression* of a sunrise over water with bold daubs of orange paint was ridiculed by critics whose description of the painting christened the Impressionist movement. Cézanne became increasingly influential himself as he developed his own style alongside the Post-Impressionist artists such as van Gogh, Gauguin and Seurat.

LITTLE DANCER OF FOURTEEN YEARS

Edgar Degas

This sculpture originally modelled in wax incorporates real artefacts such as hair, dancing shoes, gauze tutu and silk bodice. It was modelled on Marie van Goethem, a dancer at the Paris Opera, who was known to spend much of her time at the local Brasserie de Martyrs, also favoured by artists. The incorporation of real materials in the sculpture was considered very shocking at the time. It was finally exhibited, in a glass case, at the sixth Impressionist exhibition.

THE ARTIST'S SON *(detail)*, 1883/5

On 4 January 1872 in Paris, Hortense Fiquet gave birth to a boy who was registered as Paul Cézanne. The artist was an indulgent father who was very attached to his young son. As Paul grew up Cézanne began to depend upon him to help organize his affairs. He was later to become Cézanne's advisor, taking care of money matters and the sale of his pictures.

The Life of Cézanne

~1869~

Meets Hortense Fiquet, who models for him, and becomes his mistress.

Hortense moves in with Cézanne.

~1872~

Son Paul is born.

Cézanne, Hortense and Paul move to the village of Auvers-sur-Oise where Cézanne works with Pissarro.

~1874~

Exhibits with the first group exhibition of Impressionist painters.

~1877~

Exhibits 16 paintings at the third Impressionist exhibition.

~1878~

Cézanne's father threatens to cut off the artist's allowance after hearing of his son's mistress and child whom Cézanne had kept a secret from his parents.

THE ARTIST'S FATHER *(detail)*, 1866

In 1874, already two years after the birth of his son, Cézanne wrote to his parents; *'You ask me why I am not yet returning to Aix. I have already told you in that respect that it is more agreeable for me than you can possibly think to be with you, but that once at Aix I am no longer free and when I want to return to Paris this always means a struggle for me; and although your opposition to my return is not absolute, I am very much troubled by the resistance I feel on your part. I greatly desire that my liberty of action should not be impeded and I shall then have all the more pleasure in hastening my return. I ask Papa to give me 200 francs a month; that will permit me to make a long stay in Aix… believe me, I really do beg Papa to grant me this request and then I shall, I think, be able to continue the studies I wish to make.'*

FAMILY, FRIENDS & OTHERS
THE SECRET FAMILY

Cézanne relied heavily on his wealthy parents for financial support. When he moved in with his lover Hortense Fiquet he kept the relationship a secret for fear that his father would cut off his monthly allowance. Cézanne continued to rely upon the financial and emotional support of his family for many years and evidently found it difficult to break free. He secretly established his family in l'Estaque, not far from his parents home in Aix, and continued to spend time with his parents as well as with Hortense, all the time fearful that he would be discovered. Cézanne was also close to his two sisters who shared the promise of the family wealth with him after his father retired from the banking business. The secret of Hortense, and even the birth of Cézanne's son Paul, was kept from his parents but eventually they found out some eight years after Cézanne first met Hortense. Cézanne's father threatened to cut off his son's allowance, forcing Cézanne to seek support from his friends.

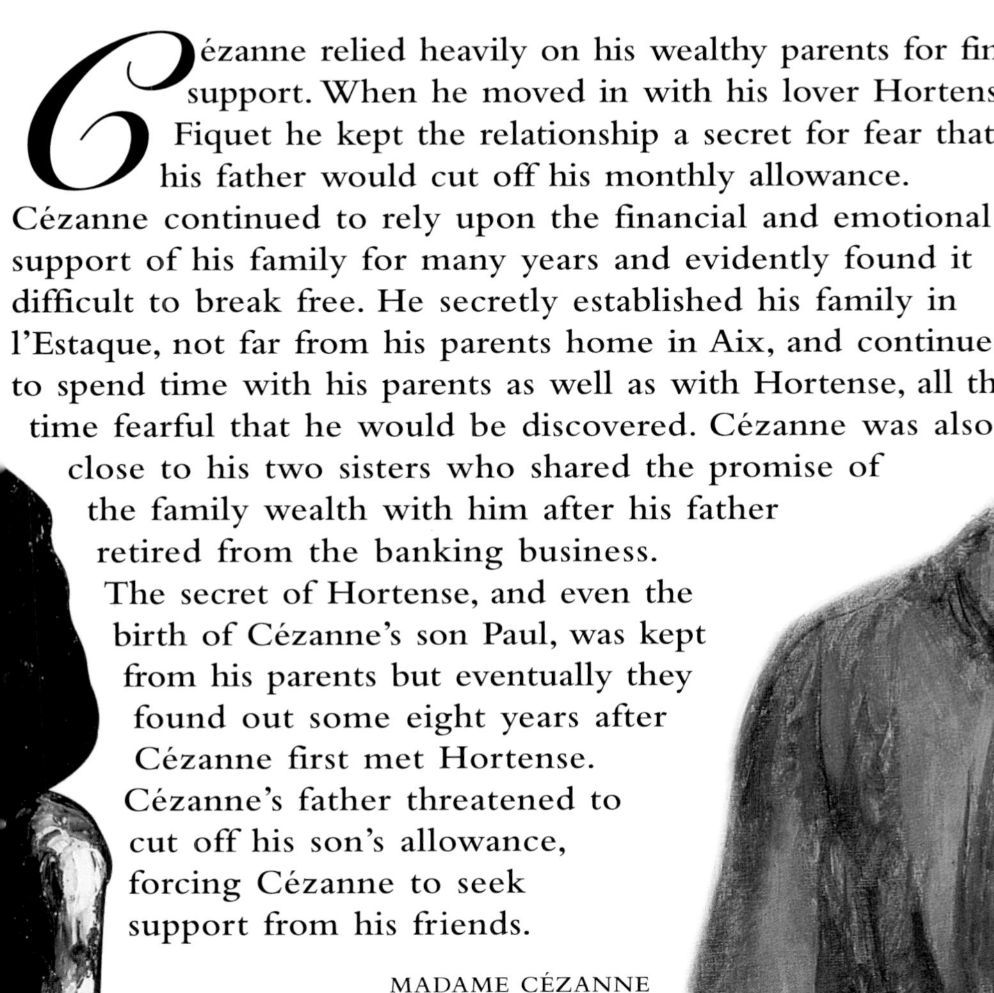

MADAME CÉZANNE IN A RED DRESS, *c.*1890

Cézanne met the 19-year-old Hortense Fiquet in Paris in 1869. Hortense was a young model described as '*a tall and handsome brunette with large black eyes*'. Cézanne, some 11 years her senior, fell in love with her and persuaded her to move in with him. They were not married until 1886, when Cézanne was 47 and his son Paul 14. Although they stayed together for many years, eventually Cézanne became indifferent to her. After his father's death Cézanne continued to live with his mother and sister Marie in Aix, while Hortense spent most of her time in Paris with their son Paul. One scornful comment gives a good picture of Cézanne's attitude; '*My wife likes only Switzerland and lemonade,*' he said.

FAMILY, FRIENDS & OTHERS

FRIENDS FROM AIX

Throughout his life Cézanne maintained friends from his home town of Aix. The 'inseparables', the childhood friends Baille, Zola and Cézanne, kept their friendship going into adulthood. Émile Zola remained very close to Cézanne until a book published by Zola in 1886 offended Cézanne to such an extent that he ceased to communicate with the writer. The acquaintances Cézanne made at the drawing school in Aix where he studied from 1856 to 1859 lasted many years. When Cézanne left for Paris in pursuit of Zola who had already decided to make a home there, he found familiar faces from Aix such as Solari and Valabrègue. These young hopefuls rubbed shoulders with the exciting avant-garde in the Parisian cafés where artists and intellectuals debated the latest artistic fashions long into the night.

THE LIFE OF CÉZANNE

~1886~
Publication of Zola's novel about a failed artist which was thought to be based on Cézanne. Their friendship breaks down.

Cézanne marries Hortense.

Cézanne inherits the family wealth after the death of his father, and moves to Jas de Bouffan, although Hortense and Paul spend most of their time in Paris.

~1895~
First one-man exhibition at Ambroise Vollard's gallery.

~1897~
Cézanne's mother dies.

~1899~
Sells Jas de Bouffan and moves into an apartment in Aix.

~1902~
Moves into a studio he has built in Chemin des Lauves in the hills outside Aix with a view of Mont Sainte-Victoire.

Zola dies.

~1904~
Works exhibited in Paris and Berlin.

~1905~
Exhibits in London with Durand-Ruel.

~1906~
Cézanne dies of pneumonia on 22 October a week after getting soaked in a thunderstorm while out painting.

~1907~
A retrospective exhibition of Cézanne's paintings is held at the Autumn Salon in Paris.

ACHILLE EMPERAIRE, *c.*1868

Emperaire was an artist from Aix who studied with Cézanne at the Académie Suisse in Paris. Cézanne was very attached to Emperaire who suffered from dwarfism. His painting portrays Emperaire's condition ruthlessly – the young man's feet are propped on a box because they would not reach the ground. However there is a sensitive handling of the face which shows Emperaire gazing thoughtfully into the distance. Emperaire stayed with Cézanne in Paris in 1872, but only for a short time. When he left he wrote; *'I have left Cézanne – it was unavoidable, otherwise I would not have escaped the fate of the others. I found him deserted by everybody. He hasn't got a single intelligent or close friend left.'* Later in life Cézanne is reported to have wanted to destroy the picture.

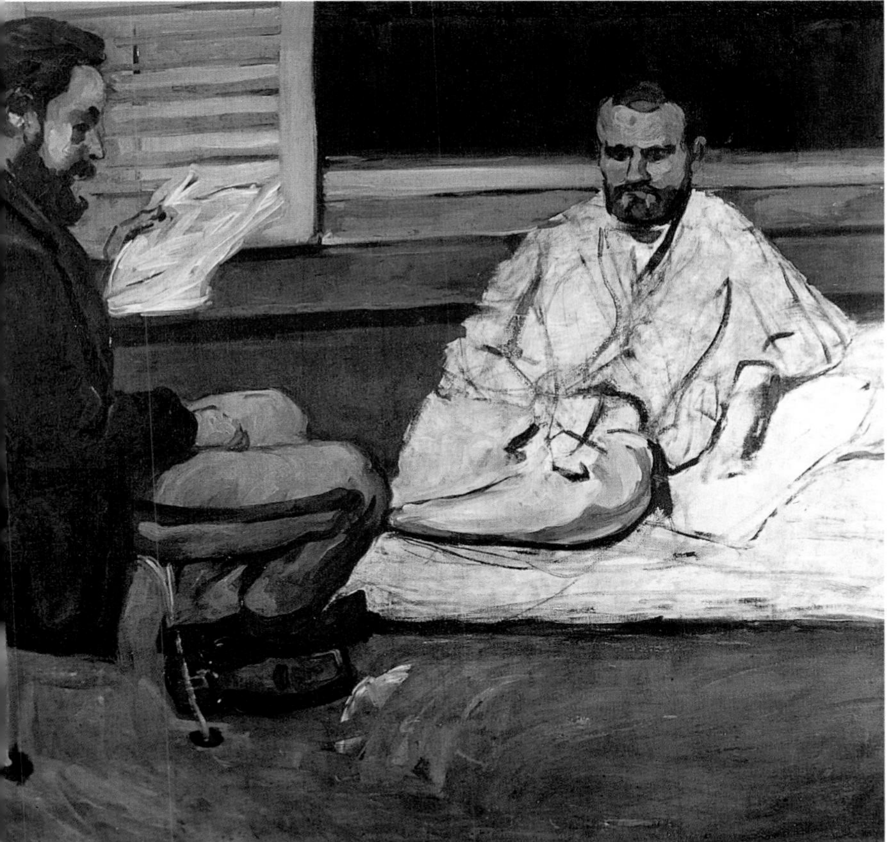

PAUL ALEXIS READING TO ÉMILE ZOLA, 1869

Zola and Cézanne had been intimate friends since childhood. Zola, a highly talented writer, became notorious for his Realist novels such as *Nana* and *Germinal,* which although causing a scandal when they were published, today are considered to be among the greatest French novels of the 19th century. This painting, found in Zola's attic after his death, is clearly unfinished, showing Zola's body as a few bold brushstrokes against the cream canvas. In 1886 Zola published a novel called *L'Oeuvre* about a failed painter named Claude Lantier. The character was said to be based on Cézanne. This caused a permanent break between the two and their friendship never recovered.

On 4 April 1886 Cézanne wrote:

> *My dear Émile*
>
> *I have just received L'Oeuvre, which you were good enough to send me. I thank the author of Les Rougon-Macquart for this kind token of remembrance and ask him to permit me to clasp his hand while thinking of bygone years. Ever yours under the impulse of past times.*
>
> *Paul Cézanne*

The letter undoubtedly refers to the relationship in the past tense and is far more formal than his normal letters to the writer. Some years later Zola said; *'Ah yes, Cézanne. How I regret not having been able to push him. In my Claude Lantier I have drawn a likeness of him that is actually too mild, for if I had wanted to tell all…!'*

JOACHIM GASQUET, 1896/7

Gasquet was a young poet from Aix and the son of one of Cézanne's childhood friends. Gasquet was very taken with Cézanne's work and set about publishing transcriptions of lengthy conversations he had with the artist. After a time their relationship became strained, as was the case with many of Cézanne's friendships.

WHAT DO CÉZANNE'S PAINTINGS SAY?

Sudden outbursts of wild painting characterized Cézanne's work in the 1860s and early 70s. It is difficult to understand how this fits with the rest of his work but when Cézanne's friend Zola wrote the controversial book *L'Oeuvre*, which was thought to be based on Cézanne, he said of Claude Lantier (the main character of the novel): '*It was a chaste man's passion for the flesh of women, a mad love of nudity desired and never possessed... Those girls whom he chased out of his studio he adored in his paintings; he caressed or attacked them, in tears of despair at not being able to make them sufficiently beautiful, sufficiently alive.*'

The black maid in attendance in Manet's painting has a far more active role in Cézanne's picture as she unveils the female figure to the man seated in the foreground.

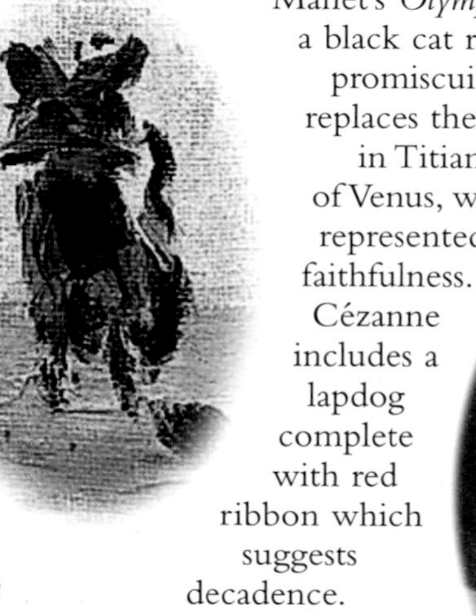

Manet's *Olympia* includes a black cat representing promiscuity. The cat replaces the dog painted in Titian's version of Venus, which represented faithfulness. Cézanne includes a lapdog complete with red ribbon which suggests decadence.

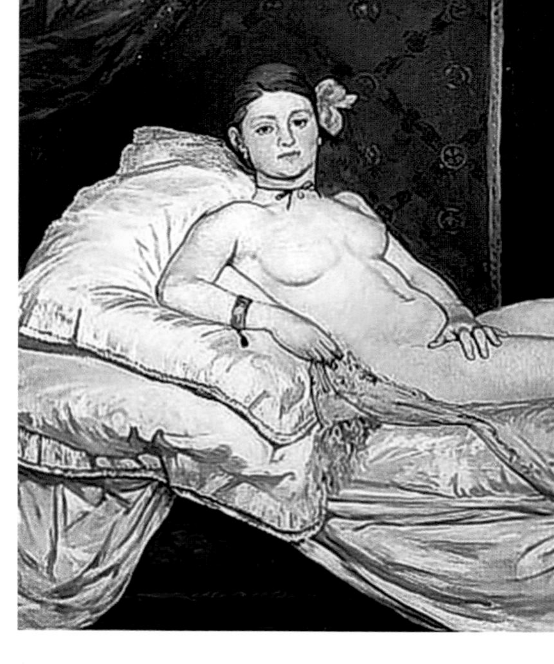

A MODERN OLYMPIA, 1873

In 1867 Cézanne made a painting which he called *A Modern Olympia.* This painting was a homage to Manet's famous painting *Olympia* which was the sensation of the 1865 Salon. Apparently the subject came up in conversation some years later when Cézanne was staying with Dr. Gachet in Auvers. The story states that Cézanne immediately took up his brushes and with uncharacteristic speed painted another canvas also called *A Modern Olympia.* This version of 1873 was exhibited at the first Impressionist exhibition in 1874. Criticism was heaped upon the exhibition. A female critic who wrote in the paper *L'Artiste* under the name Marc de Montifaud commented of *A Modern Olympia; 'On Sunday the public saw fit to sneer at a fantastic figure that is revealed under an opium sky to a drug addict. This apparition of pink and nude flesh… has left even the most courageous gasping for breath. Mr Cézanne merely gives the impression of being a sort of madman who paints in delirium tremens.'*

This man is undoubtedly a self-portrait with Cézanne's own distinct features.

OLYMPIA

Édouard Manet

Manet painted *Olympia* in 1863 but did not submit it for exhibition until 1865. Manet referred back to a well-known painting called *Venus of Urbino* painted by Titian in 1538. Manet's Olympia is a modern courtesan who is self-possessed and confident, unashamed of her nakedness. She looks directly at the viewer, thereby involving the spectator in the scene. This confrontation was shocking for the public, who were used to gazing on images of naked women safely portrayed as mythical goddesses.

Mont Sainte-Victoire 1880

WHAT DO CÉZANNE'S PAINTINGS SAY?

MONT SAINTE-VICTOIRE

The mountain of Sainte-Victoire dominates the landscape around Aix. Mont Sainte-Victoire became Cézanne's *motif*, his subject to which he continually returned, painting the landscape again and again. It is perhaps for his views of Sainte-Victoire that Cézanne is best known. In 1881 Cézanne's brother-in-law, Maxime Conil, purchased a house called Bellevue which stood to the southwest of the town of Aix. The house was situated on a hill overlooking the Arc valley with the mountain of Saint-Victoire in the distance. Cézanne visited Bellevue on many occasions, setting up his canvas to paint the rural landscape, especially the view along the valley towards the flat-topped mountain. A viaduct in the middle distance formed a bold horizontal line running towards the foot of the mountain. Cézanne loved this countryside which he had known so well since childhood. He said that the subject was *'the conformation of my country.'*

Mont Sainte-Victoire 1885

Cézanne painted Sainte-Victoire repeatedly in different conditions of light, exploring the form which appeared ever-changing under the harsh Provençal sun. However Cézanne's obsession was about making something with a strong underlying structure. He grew further and further away from the Impressionist painters whose fixation with the transient effects of light on colour was for Cézanne *'not permanent'*. In conversation Cézanne said to Joachim Gasquet; *'Impressionism, what does it mean? It is the optical mixing of colours, do you understand? The colours are broken down on the canvas and reassembled by the eye. We had to go through that… but now we need to give a firmness, a framework to the evanescence of all things.'*

Mont Sainte-Victoire 1890

Mont Sainte-Victoire was the subject Cézanne chose to create this firmness, this permanence that he felt had eluded fellow painters such as Monet. It was more than just a mountain, itself the very essence of permanence. Sainte-Victoire was the foundation of Cézanne's beloved Provence countryside, the security of his family home, the solidity of his youthful friendships.

MONT SAINTE-VICTOIRE SEEN FROM LES LAUVES

When his last link with his parents was cut after his mother's death in 1897 Cézanne was drawn nearer to the mountain, taking a studio in the hills at Chemin des Lauves overlooking Aix. This painting made between 1904 and 1906 is a view of Sainte-Victoire from Les Lauves. The same motif Cézanne was painting almost 30 years earlier became increasingly abstract, with sky and ground merging together as Cézanne searched for the underlying framework in his painting.

MOUNTAINS IN PROVENCE, 1878/80

Cézanne described how he tried to paint from nature. This description is a telling insight into the way the artist works, his thought process as he struggles to create a work of art. *'If I reach too high or too low, everything is a mess. There must not be a single loose strand, a single gap through which the tension, the light, the truth can escape. I have all the parts of my canvas under control simultaneously. If things are tending to diverge, I use my instincts and my beliefs to bring them back together again... I take the tones of colour I see to my right and my left, here, there everywhere, and I fix these gradations, I bring them together... They form lines, and become objects, rocks, trees, without my thinking about it. They acquire volume, they have an effect. When these masses and weights on my canvas correspond to the planes, and spots which I see in my mind and which we see with our eyes, then my canvas closes its fingers.'*

HOW WERE THE PAINTINGS MADE?

THE STRUCTURE OF THINGS

Cézanne was reaching for a way of painting what was beneath the surface, the basic form of his subject expressed and modelled in colour. His fellow Impressionist painters worked very quickly in order to capture the fleeting impression of light on the surface whereas Cézanne worked slowly, laboriously, using colour to build solid shapes. He is famous for his statement that he *'wanted to make of Impressionism something solid and durable, like the art of the Museums.'* He sought to create images which represented the subject as colour and tone together, that is to identify a colour which could represent the tone of an object and in this way build something solid out of colour alone, without the need for line or shade. He expressed this method of working when he said; '*I try to render perspective through colour alone... I proceed very slowly, for nature reveals herself to me in a very complex form, and constant progress must be made. One must see one's model correctly and experience it in the right way, and furthermore, express oneself with distinction and strength.*'

BEND IN THE ROAD, *c.*1900/6

Cézanne increasingly analyzed his landscapes as ordered brushstrokes and parallel colour blocks which are described today as *'constructive strokes'*. Through these building blocks of colour he attempted to represent sunlight on the landscape rather than provide an impression of its effects. Although he rejected the Impressionist style he still adopted the use of complementary colours famously used by the Impressionists, such as setting muted blues against oranges to create depth in the picture plane. It is in canvases such as *Bend in the Road* and the 1904 painting of *Sainte-Victoire* that historians have seen the beginnings of Cubist and eventually Abstract art.

PAUL CÉZANNE SITTING IN THE COUNTRY

This photograph, taken by Cézanne's friend Émile Bernard, shows Cézanne as an old man in his beloved Provençal countryside.

HOW WERE THE PAINTINGS MADE?

STILL LIFE

Cézanne said he wanted to conquer Paris with an apple – in other words to become famous for his modest still-life paintings. He applied the same methodical analysis to his still-life pictures as he did to his landscapes which often resulted in the fruit rotting in the bowl before he could finish the painting, so eventually he used artificial fruit. The simple shapes of the fruit and bowls appealed to him; they were after all the basic spheres, cubes and cylinders out of which all things can be said to be made. Another indication of the time he devoted to the paintings is the fact that sometimes contradicting shadows can be seen. Each time he returned to the subject he would paint exactly what he saw, even if the shadow had moved. He would spend weeks, sometimes months or longer on a painting, and if he was not happy with the result would abandon the picture or sometimes destroy it.

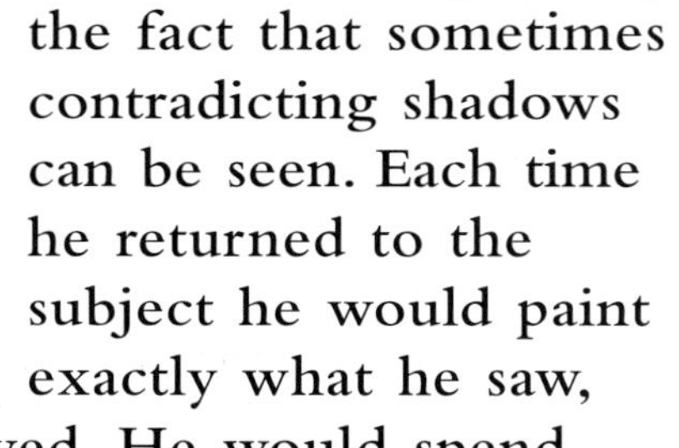

FLOWERS AND FRUITS, *c.*1880

Cézanne derived enormous pleasure from creating fruits which were painted with such delicacy of colour and yet were given real volume and weight. It is almost as if the viewer can feel their roundness in the palm of the hand.

VESSELS, BASKET AND FRUIT, 1888/90

The still-life pictures appear at first glance to be simple representations of everyday objects, and yet these paintings are some of the most sophisticated images to have been created at the end of the 19th century. The artist's viewpoint has been very carefully selected and is in fact not one but several shifting viewpoints. The objects are seen from a number of different angles at the same time, so the jug appears to be tipping forward but the plane of the table top contradicts it. The distortions of perspective are deliberate so that important shapes and colours balance each other pictorially rather than present a true representation of the still life. This playfulness broke with the rules of art which had been established for generations and stretched back to the Renaissance. Cézanne flattens the perspective where it pleases him to do so, pursuing harmony of shape and colour to create a painting which cares more for the 'abstract' elements of composition than for a perfect illusion of objects on a table.

STILL LIFE WITH CURTAIN, *c*.1898/9

This still life was carefully arranged in order to present exactly the combination of shapes and juxtaposition of colours that Cézanne wanted.

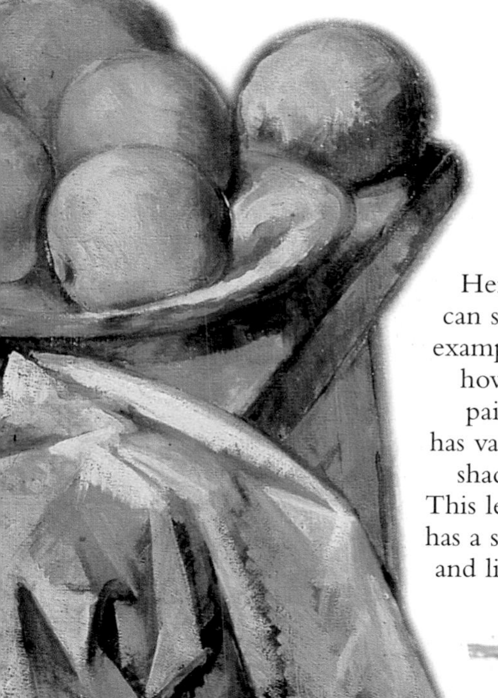

Here we can see an example of how this painting has varying shadows. This lemon has a shadow on the top, and light at the bottom.

The shadow and light are reversed here.

THE CARD PLAYERS, 1890/95

The Card Players is one of Cézanne's best-known works. Card players are a common subject for artists and many versions of such a scene existed before Cézanne set up his canvas. He made five versions of the scene in all. Rather like his still-life pictures and paintings of Sainte-Victoire he painted the subject again and again exploring variations of the theme. In one version only two players are depicted, facing each other. In another three players sit around the table while another has three players, a standing onlooker and a boy at the shoulder of the central card player.

SOMBRE COLOURS

We can tell from the simple clothes that the figures clearly belong in the Provençal countryside and their serious expressions suggest they have a hard life. This rather gloomy atmosphere is emphasized by the sombre colours used by the artist.

ABSTRACT QUALITIES OF THE IMAGE

The very symmetrical composition with eyes focused down on the cards gives the pictures a stillness which recalls Cézanne's still-life paintings. Cézanne's arrangement of people and prop-like objects is organized in a manner which deliberately sets out to present a combination of shapes and colours rather than tell the story of two men playing cards. The artist is more interested in the abstract qualities of the image than a representation of an event.

FAMOUS IMAGES

After the death of his father in 1886 Cézanne inherited a large fortune and he could have led whatever life he chose. He decided on the simple life at Jas de Bouffan, the family house in Aix, painting the surrounding countryside and whatever was close at hand. Cézanne often found models for his portrait paintings among the labourers who worked on the estate at Jas de Bouffan. He could afford to pay these workers to sit for him for long periods of time, for Cézanne was as exacting with his studies of people as he was with the still life and landscape. He painted at Jas de Bouffan, living an increasingly secluded life with his sister as well as Hortense and Paul, until he set up a new studio on the road to Les Lauves which afforded views of his favourite motif, Mont Sainte-Victoire. It appeared that Cézanne increasingly shunned contact with people, sometimes positively ducking out of sight of acquaintances he might meet in the street.

WOMAN WITH A COFFEE POT, 1890/5

It is likely that the subject for this painting was one of the servants at Jas de Bouffan, possibly the housekeeper. There is a feeling of massiveness about the form of the woman, a sense that the figure is as monumental as the mountain outside Aix that Cézanne loved to paint.

The vertical forms of the cafetière and standing spoon echo the erect pose of the woman who appears to be painted in a different plane to the table top, just as Cézanne painted conflicting perspectives in his still-life pictures.

The blues and greens of the woman's dress against the orange and burnt brown of the wall panelling and tablecloth tend to accentuate her solidity and isolate her from the background.

BATHERS, 1875/77

This is one of the earliest examples of Cézanne's paintings of bathers in the landscape.

FAMOUS IMAGES
THE BATHERS

In 1899 the Jas de Bouffan was sold and Cézanne moved into an apartment in Aix with a housekeeper. His wife and son spent most of their time in Paris, and Cézanne had a house built at Chemin des Lauves in the hills outside Aix. The house had a studio on the first floor with a ceiling some five metres high and a long narrow slit in the outer wall in order to move large canvases. Around 1900 Cézanne returned to a favourite subject, figures in the landscape. He had painted a number of paintings on this theme in the 1870s and 80s but he now concentrated on making a number of large paintings including the biggest canvas at over two metres by two and a half metres.

THE LARGE BATHERS, 1894-1905

This group of bathers comprises all female figures, like the other large bathers canvas. Cézanne did not mix male and female bathers together in his pictures, possibly for fear of creating a scene which would be considered inappropriate, and which would distract from his main purpose of using the figures as compositional devices, completely anonymous as human beings. However symbolic elements have been introduced into the picture and it is certain that Cézanne would have been aware of their meaning. The dog, curled up asleep at the foot of the picture, represents faithfulness. The fruit on the ground and in the basket represent the loss of innocence. These symbols have been used for centuries, and Cézanne himself used similar references in earlier works including *The Modern Olympia* which was based on a painting by Manet.

THE LARGE BATHERS, 1906

Cézanne spent seven years working on this painting in his methodical manner, returning to the canvas on numerous occasions in order to change aspects, or to add a little, just as he did with all his paintings. The canvas, which is now in the Museum of Art in Philadelphia, was the largest Cézanne painted. It has a strong triangular-shaped centre emphasized by the leaning figures and trees, and comprises a group of women - no men are present – who appear to be resting after bathing. The women are crudely depicted, and are more important for the structural shapes they present than for their individuality.

At the centre of the triangle on the far side of the river are two figures and behind them a church tower. One of the figures standing on the far bank is a man with his arms folded, staring across at the women. It has been suggested that this is Cézanne himself, under the shadow of the church, looking across the river at the women, at a scene he can never reach. Several of the women are staring back towards the figure. Is this a comment on his relationship with women from whom he grew more distant as life progressed?

HOW WERE THE PAINTINGS MADE?

THE BATHERS

Cézanne would draw figures from life, although he became increasingly awkward with models, especially in unclothed poses. Instead he started to rely upon memory and references taken from sketches and reproductions of paintings from the Old Masters in the Louvre and elsewhere, even sketches from illustrations in his sister's fashion magazines. One report mentions Cézanne using an album entitled *Le Nu au Musée du Louvre* (The nude in the Louvre Museum), which he bought from a shop in Paris as a reference for figure studies. Wherever Cézanne did make studies from life he would use and reuse the figure in many works, treating it as a stock item which could be called upon for a number of different purposes.

A PHENOMENAL MEMORY

For his bathers series Cézanne relied on his memory of the human form to help him create the figures. *'Painting is in here'* he said, tapping his head. Critics have found clear references in the Bathers series to known works such as Michelangelo's *Dying Slave* sculpture (above).

BATHERS

In addition to the canvases painted in oils he produced a number of pencil and watercolour sketches dominated by blues and greys. These did not serve as preparatory sketches for the oil paintings but are independent versions in their own right. Some of the watercolour and oil paintings appear unfinished because Cézanne has left areas of the paper or canvas uncovered so the base colour shows through. It is almost as if the act of filling in the canvas would have unbalanced the picture, and that the spots of white are as important as the patches of colour in creating an overall harmony. This painting demonstrates the 'hatching' brushstrokes that Cézanne frequently used, going in different directions to provide movement across the picture surface.

Cézanne in front of one of The Large Bathers

THE LARGE BATHERS, *(detail)*

This detail from the sky of *The Large Bathers* shows the way in which Cézanne applied the paint. Loose, large brushstrokes have been used to apply fairly thin coats of pigment in a very free style. The contra-angled strokes are clearly visible in this detail, and serve to animate the picture's surface when seen from a distance. The picture gives the appearance of being painted quickly although it is known that Cézanne spent literally years working on the canvas.

THE AUDIENCE FOR THE PICTURES

Cézanne exhibited with the Impressionists during the 1870s and at small shows such as Les Vingt in Brussels but did not have his own exhibition until 1895, when his work was exhibited at the gallery of Paris art dealer Ambroise Vollard. Cézanne did not need to sell his paintings to make a living as he was financially independent after the death of his father. His work was exhibited sporadically during the late 1890s and an auction of Émile Zola's art collection on his death in 1902 saw Cézanne's paintings fetch an average of 1,500 francs. The first gallery to buy his work was the Nationalgalerie in Berlin. Shortly before his death in 1906 the art world was beginning to take notice of Cézanne's work, with 30 paintings being displayed in the 1904 Paris Salon and 10 paintings being exhibited at the Grafton Street gallery in London in 1905, thanks to the efforts of dealer Durand-Ruel. In 1907, the year after Cézanne's death, a major retrospective exhibition of his work featuring 56 paintings was held at the Paris Autumn Salon.

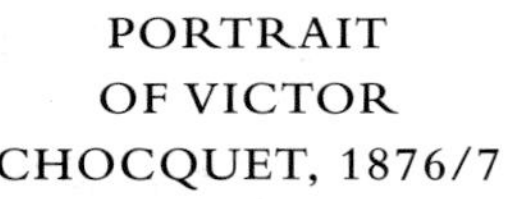

PORTRAIT OF VICTOR CHOCQUET, 1876/7

Victor Chocquet was a civil servant in the Ministry of Finance who was not wealthy, but nevertheless became a collector of art after befriending the Impressionist painters. Cézanne painted his portrait many times. Chocquet built up an impressive collection of paintings including 35 works by Cézanne.

DARK AND LEGENDARY

The art critic Gustave Geffroy (left) saw the exhibition organized by Ambroise Vollard and wrote the following; *'Passers-by walking into the Galerie Vollard, in rue Laffitte, will be faced with about 50 pictures: figures, landscapes, fruit, flowers, from which they can finally reach a verdict on one of the finest and greatest personalities of our time. Once that has happened, and it is high time it did happen, all that is dark and legendary about Cézanne's life will disappear, and what remains will be a rigorous and yet attractive, masterly and yet naive life's work... He will end up in the Louvre.'*

THE BATH, *c.*1881

Mary Cassatt

The American Impressionist painter Mary Cassatt met Cézanne in 1894 when they were both staying at Claude Monet's home town of Giverny. She describes her first encounter with Cézanne; *'When I first saw him, he looked like a cut-throat with large red eyeballs standing out from his head in a most ferocious manner, a rather fierce-looking pointed beard, quite grey, and an excited way of talking that positively made the dishes rattle... in spite of the total disregard for the dictionary of manners, he shows a politeness towards us which no other man here would have shown.'*

PORTRAIT OF AMBROISE VOLLARD *(left, detail)*, 1889

A young art dealer named Ambroise Vollard who had made contact with Cézanne through his son Paul decided to champion Cézanne's work. He arranged a one-man exhibition of Cézanne's paintings in his Paris gallery in 1895, exhibiting 50 works to a public who knew nothing of this painter from Aix.

SELF-PORTRAIT *(detail)*, 1873/6

Cézanne painted the portraits of his wife, his son, friends such as Zola and Gasquet and sometimes the servants and labourers around the family estate, but did not undertake commissions in the same way as his contemporaries such as Renoir did. Cézanne did not need the money from such commissions but also his very slow and methodical way of working did not lend itself to private sittings. The artist painted his own portrait repeatedly, one model he could guarantee would pose without problems, unlike his young son who could never stay still to the satisfaction of his father. This self-portrait was made around 1875. The critic Louis Vauxcelles described Cézanne in an article; *'Cézanne is a legendary figure with a coarse bristly face, a body wrapped in a haulier's rough woollen greatcoat. But this Cézanne is a master.'*

SUMMARY

THE INFLUENCE OF THE IMPRESSIONIST MOVEMENT

Impressionism set out to achieve greater naturalism by trying to capture the effects of light. In doing so it challenged the accepted conventions of the day. It not only became the leading artistic movement of its time, but a commercial success as wealthy American industrialists with a taste for art became collectors. The influence of Impressionism on future generations of artists was great, enabling them to push conventional art to its limits and beyond into the abstraction which dominated the 20th century.

The experimental techniques used by the Impressionists paved the way for future generations of artists, and for the development of Western art in the 20th century. Art historians point to Cézanne's search for the underlying structure in his compositions as the foundation of modern art from which Cubism and then Abstraction came. His obsession with formal elements of composition and his use of colour as tone makes his art so important to those who followed. He made it possible for artists to start questioning what they saw, the way in which they saw it, and how they interpreted and represented what was in front of them.

ENCHANTED FOREST

Jackson Pollock

The paintings of the Abstract Expressionist artist Jackson Pollock owed much to the last great water lily paintings. Both the Monet and the Pollock paintings are about the artist's feelings towards colours, space and pattern across a huge canvas. To create *Enchanted Forest*, Pollock restricted himself to a palette of gold, black, red and white, and poured, splattered and dripped paint over an unstretched canvas.

IMPRESSIONISM TODAY

Impressionism is now more popular than ever, presenting an appealing world full of warm sunlit landscapes full of figures for whom it always appears to be a slow Sunday afternoon. Impressionist pictures are reproduced all around us, for example on wall calendars and on greetings cards.

Monet found both critical and commercial success in his own lifetime, and his paintings are still very popular. Renoir's legacy too is considerable; his catalogue consists of about 6,000 pictures. Today his works can be found in the major art galleries around the world, particularly in America. The Philadelphia Art Museum held a retrospective of Cézanne's work in 1996, which drew in nearly 550,000 visitors. In 1911, the Fogg Art Museum at Harvard University staged a retrospective of Degas' work. By 1915 his pictures were hanging alongside those of Rembrandt and Rubens at the Knoedler Gallery in New York. When Degas died, it started an avalanche of demand for his work and dealers' prices rose sharply.

COLLECTORS

The Impressionists' art works continue to be highly valuable to collectors; in 1990, Renoir's *Le Moulin de la Galette* (left) sold for £48.4 million ($78.1 million) – one of the most expensive paintings ever sold. Cézanne's *Rideau, Cruchon et Compotier* sold for £36 million ($60 million) in 1999, where more recently Degas' sculpture of the *Little Dancer* (above) reached £13.3 million ($18.9 million) in February 2009. In the same month Monet's *Dans la Paraire* – a painting of his wife Camille reading in a meadow, sold for £11.2 million ($16 million), although the record auction price for one of his works remains for *Le Bassin Aux Nympheas,* selling at an astonishing £40.9 million ($67.5 million) in June 1998.

GLOSSARY

Abstract – Abstract art is based upon the idea that elements of a picture, such as colour, shape and form, have an intrinsic visual value aside from their use by artists to represent a recognizable subject.

Bas-relief – Relief is sculpture which is not free-standing but is similar to a painting with raised surfaces. The depth of the projections from the background determines the name given to a relief, normally cast in bronze or built up in plaster, clay or a similar material. High-relief (*alto-relievo*) has very deep projections compared with bas-relief (*basso-relievo*).

Belle époque – A French term to describe the period of life in the late 19th century and early 20th century up to the First World War. The belle époque (translated as 'fine period') was notable for its comfortable lifestyle free from major conflicts.

Botticelli, Sandro (1445–1510) – An extremely influential painter who lived and worked in Florence at the end of the 15th century. His best-known works, such as *The Birth of Venus*, use both pagan and Christian imagery together, and are executed in a style which was soon to be displaced by the High Renaissance style of Michelangelo.

Canvas – Artists usually painted on linen canvas, although cotton and hemp were also available. In Monet's day the canvas could be bought in standard sizes, stretched around a wooden frame and primed ready for use.

Caricature – Normally means a picture of a person, usually a drawing, but can also mean a written or acted representation. The caricature exaggerates characteristic features for comic effect.

Charcoal – This material has been used by artists for centuries and is excellent for drawing on both paper and canvas. It is made from twigs of vine or willow, which are charred by burning in a closed container without air. Charcoal has frequently been used by artists to mark out the first stages of a painting.

Composition – This word is often used as a general term meaning 'painting', however the specific meaning refers to the combination of elements in a picture which the artist strives to bring together to give an overall visual impact.

Courbet, Gustave (1819–77) – An extremely influential artist who was largely self-taught and whose art was based on the rejection of idealization and Romanticism in favour of realism which he believed was truly democratic and 'noble'. His depictions of peasants working in the fields and stone quarries were largely unpopular but his work was admired by the new generation of Impressionists who valued his rejection of the classical in favour of his depiction of the real world around him.

Ébauche – The traditional method of painting in the 19th century required the artist to draw out the picture in charcoal on the canvas, then paint the shadows and tones with a highly diluted reddish-brown colour. Coloured layers were then painted over it. This brown 'undercoat' was known as the ébauche or sauce.

Engraving – The word covers many different types of printing processes but should really only apply to the method of printing whereby lines are cut or etched into a metal plate and ink transferred from the grooves onto paper.

Expressionism – The Expressionist movement in art sought a way to express emotional force through exaggerated line and colour. Expressionist painters turned from the naturalism found in Impressionist art and attempted to create emotional impact with strong colours and simplified forms such as those found in van Gogh's work.

Hatching – This is shading by means of parallel lines on a drawing or painting. Cross-hatching is shading with two sets of parallel lines, one crossing the other. It is often used to depict shadows or dark tones rather than filling an area with solid colour.

Louvre – The most famous national museum and art gallery in France. Originally a Parisian royal palace built around 1546, it has been a venue for displaying art since 1793 and today attracts more visitors than any other museum or gallery in France.

Motif – This is a word which is used to describe a distinctive idea or theme which is continuously elaborated by the artist and applies to many kinds of art forms such as music, painting and literature. Cézanne's motif was Mont Sainte-Victoire, which he painted repeatedly during his lifetime.

Oeuvre – A French term which is used to describe the entire output of one artist. An Oeuvre catalogue, therefore, attempts to give a record of every work produced by the artist. The term can also apply to musicians and writers. Zola's book which caused a rift with Cézanne was entitled *L'Oeuvre*, and was a play on words.

Pastel – Pastels are sticks of colour which are made from compressed dry powdered pigment mixed with gum. Once pressed into moulds and set, the sticks are hard but fragile, and their colour is easily transferred when rubbed onto paper. The harder pastels are similar to chalk; softer pastels are similar to oil paints.

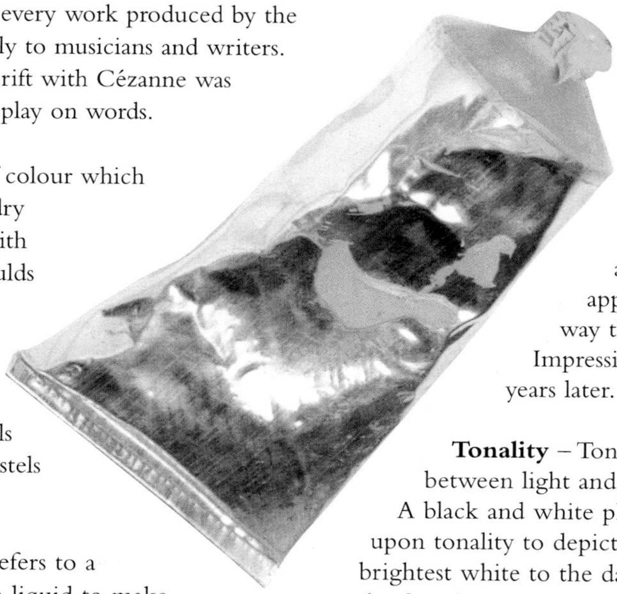

Pigment – This generally refers to a powder that is mixed with a liquid to make paint. The powder, usually made by grinding specific minerals or plants, is added to oils for oil painting but can be mixed with other mediums for different types of painting such as fresco or watercolour.

Porcelain – A ceramic material which is renowned for its translucent qualities and mainly used for manufacturing vases, cups and plates. It is made from kaolin (a type of clay) and a paste that includes substances such as soapstone and bone ash. The finished product is of fine quality and lends itself to decoration. Renoir started his career painting images on porcelain.

Rococo – This word derives from the French word *rocaille* (rock work) and is applied to a decorative style which became prominent in the early 18th century. France and Southern Germany are best known for architecture, painting and decorative arts which were made in the rococo style and which is exemplified by small curves, rounded forms and sometimes excessive ornamentation.

Romantic movement – The Romantic artists were concerned with the expression of passion and the love of the exotic, in direct contrast to those who followed Classicism. Examples of the two styles can be seen in the work of Delacroix, a Romantic, and his contemporary Ingres who painted in the Classical tradition.

Still life – The still life usually depicts a collection of objects (jugs, plates, flowers, fruit, candles etc.) which do not appear to be important in their own right but were usually chosen by the artist to symbolize more than their individual appearance. Items such as skulls, hour-glasses, candles or butterflies were often depicted to represent the transient nature of life, for example, as were certain types of flowers known for their seasonality. The tradition started in about the 16th century.

Titian (c.1490–1576) – Titian is perhaps the most famous of all Venetian artists. He was part of the high Renaissance along with Michelangelo. Towards the end of his life he developed a very free style of painting applying patches of colour in a way that seemed to anticipate the Impressionist manner more than 300 years later.

Tonality – Tonality refers to the gradations between light and dark regardless of the colour. A black and white photograph will depend entirely upon tonality to depict the subject, ranging from the brightest white to the darkest black. It is complicated by the fact that artists have to translate tonality into colour.

Venus – The Roman goddess of love, identified with the Greek goddess Aphrodite, mother of Cupid. The portrayal of the female nude in art is often referred to as Venus without a particular link to the Roman myth.

Wood block print – A wood block print is a form of engraving. If an unmarked piece of wood is covered in black ink and pressed onto paper, it will leave a solid black impression. If lines are gouged into the wood, these lines will show as a white image when the block is pressed onto paper. The block can be used to print hundreds of the same image before it will wear out.

INDEX

A

absinthe 76
Abstract art 110, 114, 122, 124
Aix-en-Provence 94, 95, 100, 109, 110
Algeria 15, 44, 45, 50
Art Institute, Chicago 33
American Art Association 32
American Civil War 69
Andrée, Ellen 51, 76
Animal Locomotion *(Muybridge, Eadweard) 6, 72, 79*
Argenteuil 14, 18, 19, 20, 27, 38, 42, 43, 47
Arnoux, Charles d'(Bertall) 35
Astruc, Zacharie 15, 43, 46
Aubert, Anne-Élisabeth 94, 100
Auvers-sur-Oise 5, 98, 102, 107

B

Baigneuse Valpinçon *(Ingres) 55*
Baille, Jean Baptiste 6, 94, 100, 102
ballet 74, 75, 76, 77, 82, 83, 84, 85, 87, 91
Batignolles group 13, 14, 15, 66, 96
Baudelaire, Charles 68
Bazille, Frédéric 13, 14, 15, 38, 39, 42, 45, 48
Belle époque 49, 124
Bellelli Family 66
Berlioz, Hector 75
Bernard, Émile 110
Bertall (Charles d'Arnoux) 35
The Birth of Venus *(Botticelli) 124*
Botticelli, Sandro 95, 124
Boucher, François 57
Boudin, Eugène 6, 10, 15, 20, 27
Butler, Theodore 17, 18

C

Café-concerts 49, 74, 75, 76
Café Guerbois 14, 46, 66, 74, 98
Cahen family 61
Caillebotte, Gustave 51, 100
camera 4, 7, 28, 75, 78, 83
Caricatures 8, 32, 35, 124
Cassatt, Mary 5, 6, 13, 91, 120
Cézanne, Louis-Auguste 94, 95, 100
Cézanne, Paul
art
exhibited 6, 99, 101, 102, 104, 105, 120, 121
influence 98, 99, 100, 120, 124
techniques 112, 113, 118–119
works
The Abduction *97*
Apotheosis of Delacroix *96*
The Artist's Father *102*
The Artist's Son *103*
The Autopsy *97*
Bathers *54, 56, 57, 90, 91, 116, 117, 119*
Bend in the Road *110*
The Card Players *114*
The Cutting *98*
Flowers and Fruits 112
The House of Dr Gachet at Auvers *98*
The House of the Hanged Man *99*
Joachim Gasquet *105*
The Large Bathers *116, 117, 119*
Madame Cézanne in a Red Dress *103*
A Modern Olympia *107*
Mont Sainte-Victoire *108–109*
Mountains in Provence *110*
Murals in Jas de Bouffan *95*
The Murder *97*
Paul Alexis reading to Émile Zola *105*
Portrait of Ambroise Vollard *125*
Portrait of Victor Chocquet *120*
Self-Portrait *107, 121*
Still Life with Curtain *113*
The Strangled Woman *96, 97*
Vessels, Basket and Fruit 113
Woman with a Coffee Pot *115*
family 94, 98, 100, 102, 103, 104–105
friends 94, 98, 99, 100, 104, 105, 106, 110, 121
photographs of 110
Cézanne, Paul (son) 102, 103, 104, 115, 121
Charigot, Aline 44, 45, 51
Charpentier, Georges 41, 61
Charpentier, Marguerite 61
Chevreul, Michel 24, 35
Chocquet, Victor 60, 120
Circus Fernando 76, 77
Classical style 40, 54, 55, 57, 59, 68, 69, 84, 86, 96, 101, 122, 123
Classicism 40, 97, 125
Clemenceau, Georges 16, 19, 22
Collège Bourbon 7, 94, 100
Les Collettes 59
Colour theory 26
Conil, Maxime 108
Courbet, Gustave 40, 41, 68, 96, 98, 124
Cubism 7, 110, 122

D

Dancers 48, 75, 82, 83, 84, 85, 91
Daudet, Alphonse 47
The Death of Maximilian *(Manet) 69*
The Death of Sardanapalus *(Delacroix) 68, 97*
Degas, Auguste 67, 68, 70
Degas, Edgar 5, 6, 7, 14, 21, 34, 42, 46, 55, 64–91, 101, 122, 123
art
composition 74, 77, 83
death 66, 75
exhibitions 69, 72, 90
observation 76, 78
perspective 77, 82, 83
women bathing and grooming 80, 81, 86–91
works (paintings)
The Absinthe Drinker *76*
After the Bath, Woman Drying Herself *89*
At the Beach *79*
Café-Concert at the Ambassadeurs *75*
The Dance Class *83*
Dancer Reading Paper *84*
Dancers Practising at the Barre *91*
Hortense Valpinçon *72*
Le Défilé *79*
Miss La La at the Circus Fernando *77*
Portrait in a New Orleans Cotton Office *70, 73*
Portrait of Friends, on the Stage *74*
Rehearsal of the Ballet on the Stage *86*
Self-portrait 66, 67, 70
Semiramis Building Babylon *69*
Standing Dancer, from Behind *87*
Standing Woman in a Bath Tub *88*
The Suffering of the City of New Orleans *6, 70, 79, 86*
Sulking *78*
The Tub *91*
Woman at her Bath *87*
Woman Combing her Hair *81*
Woman with a Vase *72*
works (photographs)
After the Bath *89*
Dancer of the Corps de Ballet *85*
Seated Nude *78*
works (sculpture)
Little Dancer of Fourteen Years *7, 72, 101, 123*

blindness 66
family and friends 66, 67, 71–73
Degas, René-Hilaire 71
Le Déjeuner sur l'Herbe (Manet) 98
Delacroix, Eugène 40, 41, 68, 69, 96, 97, 125
Desboutin, Marcellin 76
Diana bathing (Boucher) 57
Doncieux, Camille see Monet, Camille
Doria, Count Armand 99
Durand-Ruel, Paul 6, 7, 17, 22, 23, 29, 32, 33, 43, 44, 56, 62, 72, 90, 100, 104
Duranty, Edmond 14, 46, 71, 76
Duret, Théodore 43

E

ébauche 124
École des Beaux-Arts 38, 67, 94, 96
Emperaire, Achille 104
en plein air 5, 20, 29, 99
Ephrussi, Charles 51, 61
essence 87, 109
Expressionism 100, 122, 124

F

Fantin-Latour, Henri 14, 15
Fiquet, Hortense 98, 102–103
First World War 7, 19, 45
Flâneur 74–75
The Floor Strippers (Caillebotte) 100
Four Girls on a Bridge (Munch) 100
Fournaise Restaurant 45, 51
Franco-Prussian War 5, 12, 15, 32, 38, 46, 98
French Academy of Fine Arts 13
Freppa, Aurora 70

G

Gachet, Dr 48, 98, 107
Gasquet, Joachim 105, 109, 121
Gaudibert, M. & Mme. 15, 32
Gauguin, Eugéne Henri Paul 59, 100, 109
Geffroy, Gustave 120
Germinal (Zola) 105
Gervex, Henri 76
Gimpel, René 7, 19
Girardon, François 56
Giverny 7, 17, 18, 22, 30, 31, 33, 121
Gleyre, Charles 6, 14, 15, 38, 40, 42, 45, 46
Goeneutte, Norbert 49
Goujon, Jean 39

H

hatching 86, 119, 124
Herring, John 78
Hessling, Catherine (Dédée) 59
horses 78–79
Hoschedé, Alice 14, 15, 17
Hoschedé, Ernest 14, 15, 17, 32
Hoschedé, Suzanne 17

I

Impressionism 4–5, 20, 21, 32, 33, 34, 35, 42, 43, 46, 47, 50, 53, 54, 55, 56, 57, 106, 110, 122
exhibitions 4–5, 17, 21, 34, 35, 100, 123
Ingres, Jean Auguste Dominique 54, 55, 68, 72, 76, 80, 95, 96, 125
Impression, Sunrise 4, 6, 21, 24

J

Jas de Bouffan 95, 104, 115
Jeanniot, Georges 85
Juárez, Benito 69
The Judgement of Paris (Rubens) 59

L

Lacaux, Romaine 40
Legrand family 48, 60
Laporte, Emile-Henri 38
Latouche 15
Le Havre 4, 10, 11, 14, 15, 19, 21, 32
Lecadre, Jacques & wife 14
Lefranc & Company 25
Léroy, Louis 4
Les Lauves 115
L'Estaque 98, 101, 103
Levy Brothers 5
Lhote, Paul 51
The Little Dancer of Fourteen Years (Degas) 7, 72, 101, 123
London 7, 12, 15, 20, 32, 70, 72, 90, 91, 104, 120
Louvre 38, 44, 70, 96, 118, 120, 125

M

Mallarmé, Stéphane 46, 47, 62
Manet, Édouard 5, 6, 13, 14, 15, 16, 18, 29, 40, 46, 60, 66, 68, 69, 71, 74, 76, 98, 101, 106, 107, 116
Manet, Eugène 46
Manet, Julie 46
Manet, Leon 69
Manet, Suzanne 71
Matisse, Henri 6
Maximilian, Archduke 69
Meissonier, Jean-Louis 78
Merlet, Marguerite 38
Mexico 69
Monet, Blanche 30
Monet, Camille 14, 15, 16, 17, 18, 20, 27, 29, 34, 47, 123
Monet, Claude Adolphe 14, 15
Monet, (Oscar) Claude 4, 5, 6, 7, 8–35, 39, 42, 43, 44, 45, 46, 47, 56, 90, 98, 100, 119, 122, 123, 124
art 18, 28, 30, 123
caricatures 10, 32
death 19
early life 10–11, 14–15
exhibitions 17, 32
eyesight 17, 19, 30
friends 12, 13, 14–15
methods and materials 24, 27
patrons 16, 22, 33
photographs of 30, 33
plein-air painting 26–27
series paintings 22–23
water lilies 7, 19, 30, 31, 122
works
The Basin at Argenteuil 20
The Beach at Trouville 27
Boulevard des Capucines 11
Camille 34
Camille Monet on her Deathbed 16
Gare Saint-Lazare 18
Grain Stack 33
Impression, Sunrise 4, 6, 21, 24
Jean Monet 17
La Rue Montorgueil 28
Madame Claude Monet and her son 18
Morning with Weeping Willows 30–31
The Poppy Field at Argenteuil 29, 42
Portrait of Julie Manet 46
Rouen Cathedral 22–23
The Terrace at Sainte-Adresse 11, 14
The Water Lily Pond 31
The Woman in the Green Dress 34
Woman Turned to the Left 17
Women in the Garden 13, 20, 29
Monet, Jean 14, 15, 16, 17, 18, 20, 27, 28
Monet, Louise Justine 15
Monet, Michel 17, 28
Mont Sainte-Victoire 98, 104, 108–109, 115, 123
Montifaud, Marc de 107
Monotype prints 87, 88
Morisot, Berthe 5, 6, 7, 13, 21, 26, 42, 46, 56
motif 25, 39, 108, 109, 115, 125
Mulard 25
Munch, Edvard 100
Musée des Beaux Arts 70
Musson, Celestine 73
Musson, Estelle 72
Musson, Michel 73
Muybridge, Eadweard 6, 72, 78, 79

N

Nadar (Félix Tournachon) 11, 21
Nana (Zola) 105
National Academy of Design 32
Nationalgalerie, Berlin 120
New Orleans 6, 69, 70, 71, 72, 73, 81
Neo-Impressionism 34
New York 7, 17, 32, 33, 73, 90, 91, 123
Nicolaie, Louis François 32
Le Nu au Musée du Louvre 118
Nymphs bathing (Girardon) 56

O

L'Oeuvre *(Zola)* 34, 104, 105, 125
oil painting 10, 24, 25, 52, 76, 79, 87, 88, 89, 119, 125
Olympia *(Manet)* 32, 106–107, 116
opera 66, 74, 82, 101

P

Paris 5, 6, 10, 11, 12, 13, 14, 15, 17, 20, 22, 28, 29, 30, 31, 39, 38, 42, 43, 45, 46, 47, 48, 49, 51, 55, 57, 59, 60, 61, 66, 67, 69, 70, 74, 75, 76, 78, 79, 84, 90, 94, 96, 98, 99, 100, 101, 102, 103, 104, 112, 116, 118, 120, 121, 125
  artists' community 10, 13
pastels 34, 76, 81, 82, 86, 87, 88, 90, 91, 125
Perrot, Jules 83
Petit, Georges 56, 57
photography 5, 11, 21, 30, 33, 72, 76, 78, 83, 85, 89, 90, 101, 110, 125
pigments 24, 52, 57, 86, 119, 125
Pissarro, Camille 5, 6, 7, 12, 15, 21, 35, 42, 46, 56, 98, 99, 100, 101, 102
plein-air painting 4, 5, 10, 17, 20, 26, 29, 38, 47, 99
pointillism 34, 35
Pollock, Jackson 122

R

racecourse 72
railways 19, 20, 49, 98
Rand, John 24
Raphael 53, 54
Realism 5, 34, 40, 42, 47, 55, 68, 96, 97, 103, 124
Redon, Odilon 47
Renaissance 54, 66, 67, 77, 80, 113, 124, 125
Renard, Gabrielle 44, 58
Renoir, Claude (Coco) 44
Renoir, Henri 38, 39
Renoir, Jean 19, 42, 48, 59
Renoir, Leonard 38
Renoir, Pierre (artist's son) 45
Renoir, Pierre Auguste 4, 6, 7, 11, 12, 14, 18, 19, 21, 38–63, 76, 98, 100, 121, 123, 125
  art 49, 62–63
    porcelain painting 41, 42, 47, 56
    styles
      classical 40, 54–57
      dry period 44, 53, 54–55
      Impressionism 44–45, 46, 50, 52
      late style 58–59
      realism 42–43
    training and early work 40–41, 42, 44–45, 46
  exhibitions 44, 46
  family and friends 38, 43, 44, 45, 46–47
  illness and death 46, 47, 57, 59
  patrons 43, 44, 60–61
  pictured 38, 59
  works
    The Blonde Bather 7, 54
    Bather in a landscape – Eurydice 55
    Bather with long hair 58
    The Bathers 54, 56–57
    Bathers in the Seine (La Grenouillère) 39
    Bust of Madame Renoir with Pierre 45
    The Clown 44
    Country footpath in the summer 43
    Dancing at the Moulin de la Galette 49
    Déjeuner à Berneval 44
    Esmeralda dancing with a goat 42
    Gabrielle et Jean 44
    Gabrielle with jewel box 44
    The Great Bathers 56
    Lise 43
    Luncheon of the Boating Party 50–51
    Madame Alphonse Daudet 47
    Madame Charpentier 61
    Monsieur and Madame Bernheim 61
    Le Moulin de la Galette 7, 48, 49, 50, 123
    Nude in the sunlight 62
    Pink and blue 61
    Portrait of Claude Monet 47
    Portrait of Delphine Legrand 60
    Portrait of Julie Manet 46
    Portrait of Richard Wagner 47
    Portrait of Romaine Lacaux 40
    The Seine at Argenteuil 47
    The Umbrellas 18
    Woman of Algiers 41
    Young girls at the piano 7, 44, 63
    Young woman with a fan 50
Renoir, Victor 38
Restaurant Fournaise 45, 51
Rivière, Georges 49
rococo style 40, 57, 125
Roger-Marx, Claude 63
Romanticism 40, 41, 55, 68, 96,124, 125
Rottenburg, Château de 16
Rouart, Henri 88
Rouen Cathedral 22–23
Les Rougon-Macquart *(Zola)* 105
Roujon, Henri 63
Royal Society of British Artists 32
Rubens, Peter Paul 59, 123
Ryerson, Martin 33

S

Sainte-Adresse 11, 14
Salon 4, 5, 6, 13, 15, 20, 21, 29, 34, 35, 42, 43, 44, 60, 69, 70, 90, 96, 98, 100, 104, 107, 120
Salon des Refusés 12, 13, 98
Samary, Jeanne 51
San Rocco di Capodimonte 66, 71
The School of Athens *(Raphael)* 53
Seurat, Georges 34, 35, 101
Signac, Paul 34
Sisley, Alfred 5, 6, 7, 11, 12, 21, 33, 38, 42, 44, 45, 63, 100
Société anonyme cooperative d'artistes peintres, sculpteurs, graveurs 21
Société Anonyme des Artistes 42
Solari, Emile 104
A Steeplechase *(Herring)* 78
still life 71, 96, 112–113, 115,125
The Stone-breakers *(Courbet)* 41
Symbolism 59, 96, 116, 125

T

Titian 80, 88, 106, 107, 125
Tournachon, Félix (Nadar) 11, 21
Trehot, Lise 41, 43, 44
Trouville 10, 20, 27
The Turkish Bath *(Ingres)* 80

U

Utamaro, Kitawaga 80

V

Valabrègue, Antony 104
Valpinçon, Edouard 69, 70, 72
Valpinçon, Hortense 72
Valpinçon, Paul 72
van Gogh, Theo 90
van Gogh, Vincent 18, 100, 101, 124
Vauxcelles, Louis 121
Venus of Urbino *(Titian)* 107
Vidal, Pedro 48
Les Vingt 120
Vollard, Ambroise 7, 104, 118, 120, 121

W

Wagner, Richard 47
Whistler, James 56, 101
Wings at the Opéra House *(Beraud)* 75
Wolff, Albert 62
Woman Combing her Hair *(Utamaro)* 80
Women of Algiers *(Delacroix)* 40

Z

Zola, Émile 6, 14, 15, 34, 35, 46, 47, 61, 68, 81, 94, 100, 104, 105, 106, 120, 121, 125